71776

UPHOLSTERING

UPHOLSTERING

Malcolm Flitman

B T Batsford Limited   London

© Malcolm Flitman 1972

First published 1972

Reprinted 1972
Reprinted 1974
ISBN 0 7134 2753 1

Filmset by Keyspools Ltd, Golborne, Lancs
Printed and bound in Great Britain by
Tinling (1973) Ltd, Prescot, Merseyside
a member of the Oxley Printing Group
for the publishers
B T Batsford Limited
4 Fitzhardinge Street, London W1

CONTENTS

ACKNOWLEDGMENT

PREFACE

I would like to thank everybody who has helped and encouraged me in the writing of this book. In particular my family, including my uncle, Maurice Lee, as well as Bridge Upholstery (Leeds) Limited, the firm for which I am working, and Phil Weinstock, a director, who has advised me throughout.

I thank the lecturers and students of the Diploma Group at the London College of Furniture where I have been studying; Vitaluxan Limited and W. E. Rawson Limited who kindly gave up their time to talk to me and show me around their factories; General Foam Products Limited for their information about bonded chipfoam; The British Rubber Manufacturers' Association Limited for allowing me to reproduce drawings from their *Latex Foam Handbook*; Progress Mercantile Company Limited for information about rubber webbing; Eastman Machine Company Limited for information and photographs on sewing machines; Unerman Greenman Berger for information about tack trim, and the numerous other firms who sent me literature about their products.

Photographs by courtesy of Bridge Upholstery (Leeds) Limited.

Leeds 1971   MF

Within the past few years upholstery production methods have been simplified to such an extent that the student can safely tackle most upholstery jobs knowing that a professional finish can be obtained.

Due to scientific advancement the range of plastics articles being used in upholstery is continually widening. The untrained upholsterer can utilize these new materials simply and economically to help him make a neat and clean job.

This book is aimed primarily at students of upholstery who are studying towards examinations in the subject. The home handyman should nevertheless be able to use the book to full advantage by extracting the necessary information that is required for his particular job.

Chapter 8 deals with processes which are common to the chapters following, and reference will frequently need to be made back to this general chapter.

Different methods of upholstering pieces of furniture are described step by step, from the preliminary cutting of the fabric, through to the finishing off of the upholstery.

Modern and traditional upholstering methods have been dealt with simultaneously, so that a close comparison can be made to the merits of both systems.

1 TOOLS

Magnetic tacking hammer

This is the most basic of all upholstery tools. There are two main types.

1   A hammer with a plain 12 mm ($\frac{1}{2}$ in.) diameter head at one end, and an 8 mm ($\frac{3}{8}$ in.) diameter magnetized cabriole head at the other. The cabriole head is smaller and is used in places which are difficult to locate with the larger head. The unmagnetized head is also useful for nailing.

2   A hammer with a magnetized head at one end and a tack removing claw at the other end. Care should be taken not to damage the fabric when using this claw.

1   Magnetic tacking hammer

Tacks are still traditionally held in the mouth for convenience. The beginner may be put off by the danger of swallowing one, but this risk is minimized if only about six are held at one time and they are stored beneath the tongue, to be brought forward as required. Each tack can be withdrawn directly from the mouth on to the magnetized end of the hammer provided the tack is turned by the tongue so that the head faces outwards from the mouth. Accuracy in placing comes with practice.

Staple gun

This is used by manufacturers for speeding up production. It is not necessary for the home upholsterer. Guns are obtainable either air powered from a compressor, or they can be plugged in to the normal electricity mains.

Tape

A flexible 2 m (6 ft) metal tape is required for general upholstery work. One which is graduated in both metric and imperial units will be useful in helping the reader to convert from one system to the other. The reader should accustom himself to think directly in metric rather than convert continuously between the scales.

A straight wooden rule is more convenient for cutting fabric on a flat table.

Pincers

A pair of pincers is required for extracting nails and staples when stripping a frame.

Shears

A pair of shears is necessary to cut out fabric and for general upholstery work. Heavy duty shears for cutting fabric are usually 300 mm (12 in.) long but a pair 250 mm (10 in.) is suitable for both operations. It is worth investing in a pair with a good brand name.

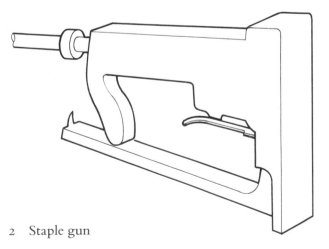

2   Staple gun

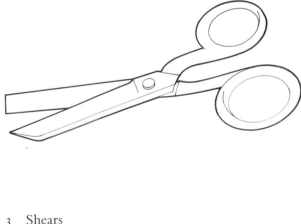

3   Shears

Bench or trestles

A bench, or a pair of trestles, is required to support the work at a height suitable for easy working, usually about 700 mm (28 in.) from the ground. The bench size should be about 750 mm (30 in.) square, and the trestles about 750 by 200 mm (30 in. by 8 in.). A padded roll is often tacked round the perimeter of the trestles to prevent damaging the work.

Mallet and ripping chisel

The ripping chisel is used for extracting tacks. Although there are many types available, an ordinary screwdriver with a plastic or wooden flat-topped handle will serve the purpose adequately. A mallet should always be used with the chisel to prevent damaging the handle.

Hold the blade on the edge of the tack head and hit the chisel handle with the mallet. A few blows may be required before the tack is lifted. The tack should be ripped out in the direction of the grain to avoid splitting the timber.

4   Trestle

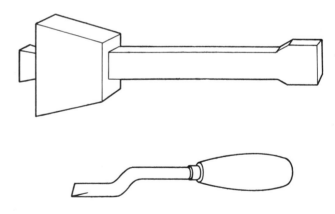

5   Mallet and ripping chisel

Staple extractor

Because of the ease with which staples can be put into a frame, there are usually more of them to extract than if tacks had been used. There are many tools available for extracting staples. The one illustrated is one of the more successful types. It works by prizing the staple up with one of the end points. A final twist pulls the staple free.

Webbing stretcher

This is used for stretching webbing tightly on a seat or back. There are several types available. If the stretcher is needed infrequently, a plain block of wood can be used. The webbing is wound around the block which is then levered against the frame to strain the webbing. Other specially made stretchers have grooved edges which fit against the rail to prevent the stretcher from slipping. One type uses a metal lever to hold the webbing, while the bat type has a slot through which the webbing is held by means of a peg. Another type has a series of spikes at one end by which the webbing is held. The disadvantage of the latter is that webbing is wasted due to the damage caused by the spikes.

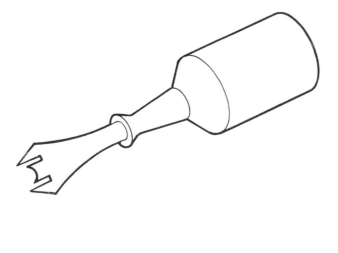

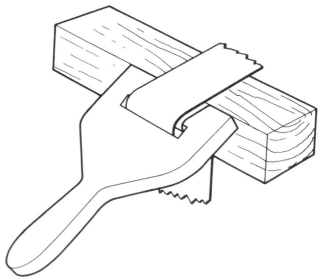

6   Staple extractor

7   The webbing stretcher in use

Needles

There are four basic types of needle required by the upholsterer.

1 *Regulator* This is used to even stuffing. It should not be used over a fabric because holes may result. Skewers are safer for this purpose as they produce smaller holes, but care needs to be taken. The flattened end of the regulator can be used for moving stuffing beneath a fabric where a hand can not reach. The needles come in different lengths, but one 250 mm (10 in.) long should be adequate.

2 *Skewers* These are not only used for regulating, but also for temporarily holding material in position before slip stitching. They are also used when making a spring edge for attaching the scrim to the edge wire prior to sewing.

3 *Straight stitching needle* This is used for stitching edges, and for threading buttons through the upholstery. Both ends of the needle are pointed.

A *bayonet needle* is similar, but is triangular in section down one third of its length. The purpose of this needle is to cut through stuffing which a stitching needle cannot penetrate. It can be obtained in different lengths, but one stitching needle about 300 mm (12 in.) long is satisfactory for most purposes.

4 *Circular needle* This is semi-circular and is used when the stitching needle is not practical, such as for sewing hessian around a spring unit. This needle is about 100 mm (4 in.) long, but smaller ones used for slip stitching are about 50 mm (2 in.) long.

A *spring needle* is bayonet pointed, and is used, as its name implies, for sewing hour glass springs to webbing. This, too, is used for sewing through stuffing which an ordinary circular needle cannot penetrate.

Button making machine

This machine converts a two-piece metal mould and a disc of fabric into a button. The top half of the mould forms the shape of the button and the lower half contains the fixing. This may be by a metal loop, a cloth tuft or a spike.

A pedal operated machine can be used more efficiently than a hand machine. The object of both types is to bring the moulds together, trapping the fabric between them. Automatic electric machines are being used increasingly in factories.

Buttons can be obtained in different sizes, ranging from small ones suitable for deep buttoning work, to the larger ones of which very few are needed for each job.

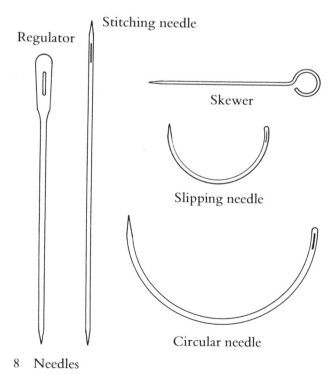

Regulator Stitching needle Skewer Slipping needle Circular needle

8 Needles

Loose seat machine

This is used in mass production to simplify the upholstering of dining chair type loose seats. The machine consists essentially of a *jig* to hold the frame, and a *ram* to compress the stuffing.

The cover is placed upside down in the machine, followed by the stuffing, and then the base which, if necessary, has been previously covered with webbing and hessian. The ram, which usually works by compressed air, is brought down. This presses the frame on to the stuffing. All that is now required is to tack or staple the overhanging cover to the frame.

Cushion filling machine

This machine was common when spring interior cushions were used. Now the use of *dacron* in cushions has created again a demand for the machine. It can be worked manually by handles or it can be air or electrically powered. The cushion is placed in the machine and the lid is closed. The sides of the cushion are compressed by the machine and the cover is slipped over the mouth of the machine. A ram then forces the cushion forward into the cover. The filling of the cushion is completed by hand.

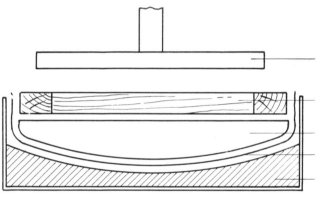

Ram

Frame covered with webbing and hessian
Foam

Fabric

Jig, cut to the shape of the foam

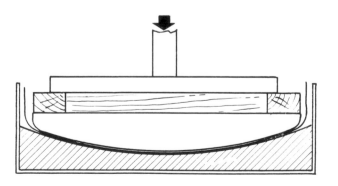

9 A loose seat machine

The cover is now stapled along the edge of the frame

Electrical cutters

Special cutters can be obtained to cut anything from flexible foams to layers of fabrics.

There are two main types of electrical cutter.

1   The *straight knife* which operates by the oscillation of a vertical blade, and can cut greater thicknesses than the round knife but is slightly slower.

2   The *round knife* which cuts by the rotation of a circular cutting wheel, is usually fitted with an automatic knife sharpener.

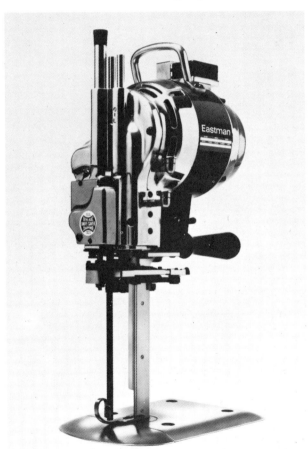

10   Straight knife

11   Round knife

2 MATERIALS

Tacks

There are two types of tack: 1 *improved* and 2 *fine*. Improved tacks are stouter, and are used where greater holding power is necessary, such as for tacking webbing and hessian. Fine tacks are used mainly on fabric.

Both types of tack can be obtained in a variety of sizes, from 6 mm ($\frac{1}{4}$ in.) which are used on thin plywood facings, to 15 mm ($\frac{5}{8}$ in.) which are used on webbing, and where many thicknesses of material are to be penetrated. Rail thickness should be taken into account when choosing tack sizes, because too large a tack may split a narrow rail.

Gimp pins

These are obtainable in different colours to match a fabric. They are 12 mm ($\frac{1}{2}$ in.) long and are cut with a small head to be inconspicuous in use. They are used for fixing cover along the edge of a show wood frame, such as may be found at the top of a chair leg. They are also used for fixing gimp in place.

Nails

1 *No-sag nails* These are used for fixing serpentine spring clips to the frame. They are 21 mm ($\frac{7}{8}$ in.) long and are serrated down their length to prevent them loosening in use.

2 *Clout nails* These are 25 mm (1 in.) long and are much thicker than no-sag nails. They are blue, have serrations down their length and are used mainly for fixing spring units to the frame.

Twines

These are made mainly from flax and hemp, but synthetic twines are gaining popularity for certain purposes where a greater strength is needed such as for fixing buttons.

1 *Stitching twine* was originally used for stitching roll edges but it can be used wherever a thin but strong twine is required such as for fixing buttons.

2 *Spring twine* is thicker and stronger than stitching twine. Its original use was for sewing loose springs to webbing but is now used more widely.

3 *Laid cord* is not frequently used. It is a thick cord for lashing springs together to form an integral unit. It is made by laying the fibres side by side to prevent the cord from stretching.

4 *Piping cord* is used in making upholstery with self-piped seams. The cord is attached to strips of the fabric, which is then sewn to the main fabric panel. See CHAPTER 7 page 48. Piping cord is made from synthetic fibres, cotton and compressed paper, in different diameters and with different stiffness ratios for different types of fabric.

Webbing

This is used as a platform to support hour glass springs and other fillings. It is not being used as widely as in the past owing to new springing systems which are available.

There are two main types of webbing.

1 *Brown webbing* which is made from jute in a plain weave and can be obtained in rolls of different widths.

2 *Black and white webbing* which is more expensive but is of better quality. It is made from flax, woven with a twill weave.

Hessian

This is a loosely woven jute cloth used for covering springs, loose stuffings and webbing. It is also used for making flies (which are extension pieces, sewn to a fabric, and are hidden inside the upholstery, therefore saving material). Hessians are available in different weights, the heavier hessians being known as *tarpaulins*.

When fitting hessian, keep warp and weft lines straight, as with a fabric. Hessian can be cut in a straight line by withdrawing a thread and cutting along this line. All hessian edges should be turned over for tacking, unless neatness is of more importance than strength, in which case they should be folded in.

Scrim

This is also made from jute. It is similar to hessian except that it has a more open weave and the threads are flat in cross section as opposed to the hessian's round threads. It is generally lighter than hessian. It is used for covering the first stuffing through which a stitched edge is sewn. Keeping the lines straight on the scrim aids the stitching of a straight edge because one thread can be followed as a guide for the line of stitching.

Calico

This is a light, bleached cotton fabric. Strips of calico are used for attaching foam to a frame and as a base cover for upholstery. It is also used for covering upholstery prior to fitting the fabric, as described under *Sewing a spring edge* page 65.

Rubber webbing

This is a form of springing, as opposed to the webbing previously mentioned. It consists of a core of rubber sandwiched between two layers of rayon cord which have been cut on the bias (diagonally). When the webbing is stretched, the cords control the amount of elongation in the webbing and, as the cords draw closer together, the webbing retains its strength. By varying the internal arrangements of cords, rubber and the angle of cut, it is possible to alter the characteristics of webbing.

All-rubber webbings are also available but, as they have no woven reinforcement, they do not retain their strength when stretched. They give a greater deflection of the cushion than reinforced webbing.

Different webbings have different characteristics. By selecting the appropriate type, the required degree of resilience can be obtained. The depth of spring can be determined by:

(a) controlling the initial tension on the webbing
(b) using a specified width of webbing
(c) adapting the spacing of the webbing to conform with the loading on specific points.

The type and thickness of the cushion should conform with the characteristics of the base.

1 *Fitting rubber webbing* There is wide scope for individual ingenuity when applying webbing to produce seats and backs which can be adapted anthropometrically to the user. Webbing which is applied from front to back on a seat has the advantage that the width, and therefore the weight of the sitter, is distributed across all the straps by the cushion. The cushion is also free to rise and fall between the sides of the frame without being tilted inwards around the sitter.

Disadvantages of this method are that a soft front edge can not be obtained, and the support given by the webbing is no greater at the points of maximum load than in less loaded areas.

Webbing stretched from side to side can be given a soft front edge; and as the zone of heaviest load occupies the rear half of the seat, increased support can be incorporated in this area, by giving the straps greater initial tension or by using wider or more closely spaced straps. Where additional support is needed the straps can be run in both directions.

Fitting straps on the back can be treated in a similar manner. Loads encountered here are less than on a seat. When the webbing is placed from side to side it is possible to provide firmness for the lumbar region and the head rest while retaining greater softness in other parts of the back. Concave backs can be made by using cross webs in low tension, pulled into shape by verticals under higher tension.

Webbing can be obtained in a continuous roll and can be applied by direct tacking or stapling. It should not be turned over at the ends. There are many types of clips available for attaching webbing to both wooden and metal frames. These clips are responsible, to a greater extent, for the successful introduction of the webbing because they simplify its application. The neatest and most popular clip is the one which fits into a grooved rail and ensures equal tension on all straps.

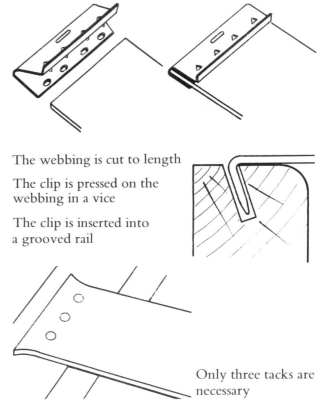

The webbing is cut to length

The clip is pressed on the webbing in a vice

The clip is inserted into a grooved rail

Only three tacks are necessary

12   Rubber webbing

13   Fixing rubber webbing

2 *Rubber platforms* These are a variation to rubber webbing. They are made from a synthetic rubber, and provide the newest form of springing system. They can be obtained in different sizes, and are attached to the frame at four points. The platform is fitted under a tension of between 8 to 15% in order to function correctly. This percentage has to be worked out when calculating the size of platform required.

Spring systems

1 *Loose hour-glass springs* This is a traditional type of spring which was used in all sprung upholstery before 1920. Its use is associated with traditional hand stitched work which is very expensive in labour. The springs are double cone in form and are made from copper-plated wire. The springs are coiled and knotted at both ends by machine.

2 *Patent spring units* These are assembled units, available for seats, backs and arms. They have a flexible wire mesh surface into which conical springs are threaded. The mesh may have a framing of rigid wire. The single cone springs are riveted to steel laths at the base of the spring. Some units are fitted with tension springs which are fixed at intervals between the cone springs and are attached to steel strips between the laths. Tension springs provide added comfort to the unit.

Double spring units are not very popular, but they give added luxury to a seat. The base layer of springs is similar to the single spring unit, but the upper

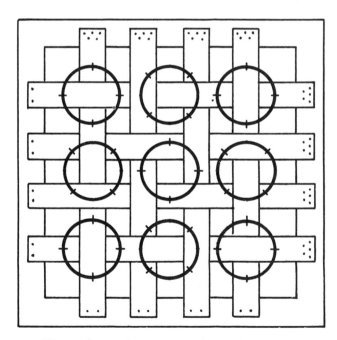

14   Hour-glass springs on a webbing base

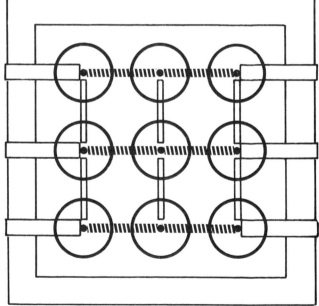

15   Spring unit

layer contains hour glass springs which may or may not be covered in calico or hessian pockets to muffle any spring noise.

3   *Tension springs*   These are suitable for seats and backs where the design does not allow for a full spring unit. Although rubber webbing is a strong competitor to tension springs, they are still being widely used. The plain metal spring is used where they are to be covered by upholstery, but when they are exposed or in contact with a cushion, they can be obtained with a PVC or woven fabric covering. They are supplied in 1·22 to 2·03 mm SWG (14 to 18 gauge) wire, and in a variety of lengths. They are fitted under slight tension, usually between 35 mm to 50 mm (1½ in. to 2 in.) on an 450 mm (18 in.)

length. The tension on these springs has an opposite mechanical action to the compression which coil springs undergo. Tension springs are fitted by direct nailing, hooking around nails, fixing to metal plates and by nailing them into a groove.

Direct nailing

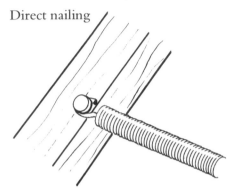

Metal plate fixing

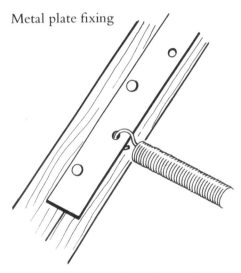

To be used only where the springs are permanently covered

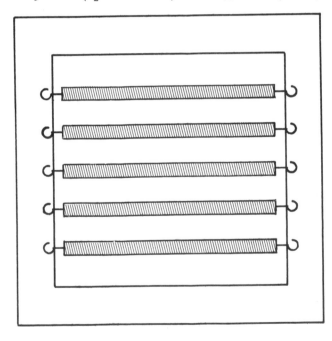

16   Tension springs

17   Fixing tension springs

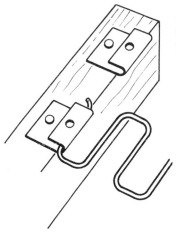

Allow the slip to hang over the rail by about 3 mm ($\frac{1}{8}$ in.)

19   Common clip used for fixing serpentine springs to a wooden frame

4   *Serpentine or no-sag springs* Serpentine springs can be supplied cut to length, in a continuous roll or made up into units. A thicker gauge spring should be used on the seat than on a back. They do not exist as a spring until they are uncoiled and fixed to the frame. They are constantly trying to return to their original circular form which gives them a permanent arc.

Five springs fixed from front to back or bottom to top, are normally used in chair seats and backs. They are fixed to the frame by means of special clips of which there is a variety for different applications. Connecting links can be used to join the springs together so that they perform as a single unit. If connecting links are not available, the springs should be tied together with a thick twine across the centre of the springs.

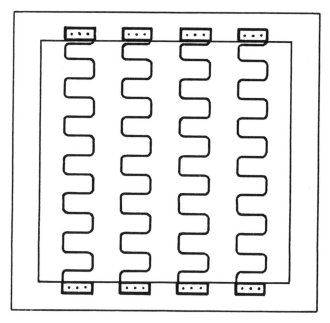

18   Serpentine springs

5   *Pullmaflex suspension unit*   This is another recent springing system which is suitable for seats and backs. It consists of a *flexolator*, a wire platform cross gridded with twisted kraft paper centre ropes, which is fastened to the frame by tension springs. They are quick and easy to fix by means of anchors which are attached to the tension springs. Only thin upholstering is required over this spring.

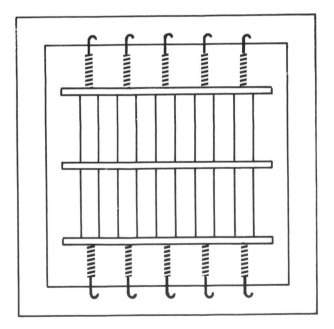

20   Pullmaflex suspension unit

Flexible foams

The manufacture of latex foam

Natural latex, containing the rubber molecule *polyisoprene*, is obtained from the rubber tree, and once was the only source of rubber. Today, synthetic rubber, *styrene butadiene latex*, is usually blended with natural latex to extract the best properties of both types of foam.

Natural latex is obtained as a juice from the *hevea brasiliensis*, the rubber tree which is cultivated in Malaysia, Indonesia, Ceylon, West Africa and Brazil. After extracting the latex by tapping the tree, ammonia is added to the latex to prevent it from drying. The latex is concentrated by extracting water, which accounts for about 65% of the liquid tapped from the tree. The latex is shipped to the site where it is to be manufactured. Ammonia is extracted by blowing air through the latex. There are two main processes of manufacture.

The first process mechanically foams the latex before it is poured into the moulds. Various chemicals are dispersed in water and are then mixed with the latex. The most important of these chemicals is sulphur, a yellow solid, which, later in the process with the action of heat, brings about the change known as *vulcanization* or *curing*. The sulphur causes the latex molecules to crosslink, which prevents the latex from becoming soft and loosing its shape during hot weather, and going hard in cold weather. Other chemicals mixed in are *soap* which helps with the foaming, and *anti-oxidants* which protect against oxygen in the air. The mixture is then allowed to mature under controlled time and temperature.

After maturing, *foaming* takes place. Foaming is continuous, by passing the mixture with air through a mixing head. The action through the rotor causes the air to be uniformly mixed with the foam. Various degrees of firmness can be produced at this stage. The foam passes through a hose to where an operator fills the moulds. *Gelling* or solidification of the foam in the mould is brought about by two additives, *zinc oxide* and *sodium silicofluoride*, which are added after frothing the foam. It is during gelling that the air bubbles are interconnected.

The moulds pass through a steam chamber for 25 minutes, which causes the sulphur to vulcanize the rubber. The foam cushion is extracted from the mould, washed, dried and inspected.

An alternative method of foaming is by chemical means. The latex compound is foamed by oxygen which is extracted from the chemical hydrogen peroxide. A calculated quantity of *hydrogen peroxide* and a *catalyst* (a substance which helps the chemical reaction to occur without undergoing change itself) are stirred into the latex compound, and this is immediately poured into a mould. Decomposition of the hydrogen peroxide with subsequent foaming of the latex compound takes place after the mould is closed. Freezing, gelling by carbon dioxide gas, and vulcanization are carried out as before.

Cavity design in latex foam
Latex foam can be obtained either plain or with cavities. Solid foam contains much rubber which serves no useful purpose. Large communicating

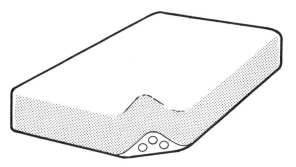

21   Non-reversible unit

22

cavities are included to increase the comfort of a cushion. This is because when sitting on a solid sheet of latex, air is driven out and it eventually feels hard. In cavity cushion, the weight is taken by the walls of the cavities, causing them to flex slightly. Cavities are made by building plugs into the lid of the mould. The design and layout of cavities control the hardness of the foam, and it is possible to provide different hardnesses in different parts of a foam block.

Types of latex foam
There are five main types of moulding, each group of which covers a range of standard products. Special mouldings can be produced when the quantity ordered justifies the making of a mould. When this is uneconomic handbuilding is used.

1   *Non-reversible units*   These have a smooth surface with the underside showing the cavities. There is a wide range of mouldings which are used for fixed upholstery work.

2   *Reversible units*   Made from two non-reversible units which are bonded together with the cavities on the inside. They are used for loose cushions. A wide range of standard mouldings are available.

3   *Cavity sheet*   Made in sheets up to 1800 mm by 1400 mm (6 ft by 4 ft 6 in.) and from 25 mm to 100 mm (1 in. to 4 in.) in thickness. They are available with various degrees of firmness and are used mainly for handbuilding.

4   *Plain sheet*   In sheet sizes up to 1800 mm by 1400 mm (6 ft by 4 ft 6 in.) and from 12 mm to 30 mm ($\frac{1}{2}$ in. to $1\frac{1}{4}$ in.) in thickness. They are available in various degrees of firmness, and are used for covering arm pads, dining chairs, bar seating and handbuilding.

5 *Pin core cavity* A one piece reversible cushion can be cut from a moulded block. The pin core pattern is uniform throughout its interior, and has an even smooth surface. It is good material for hand-building.

Properties of latex foam

1 It has an excellent rate of recovery from deformation and retains its shape and load carrying capacity for many years.

2 Firmness is controlled by the size and distribution of cavities.

3 Interconnecting open cells keep the foam ventilated and at an even temperature.

4 It is succeptable to light aging, so it should be stored away from direct light. Normal upholstery fabrics give suitable protection.

5 It is resistant to bacterial attack. It is also dust free, which benefits people who have certain allergies.

6 It can be cut easily and glued for conversion by handbuilding.

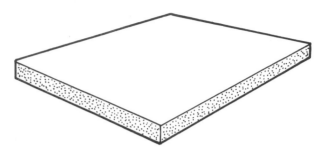

23 Plain sheet latex

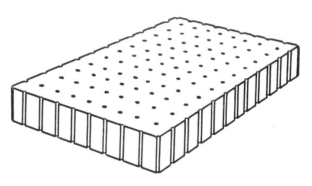

24 Pin core cavity

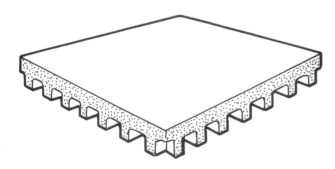

22 Cavity sheet latex

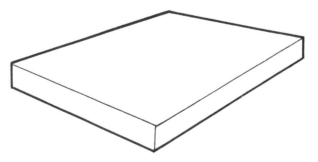

25 Polyether foam

Polyether foams

These are open cell *flexible polyurethane ether* foams as opposed to the *polyurethane ester* foams which are not used in similar flexible form in upholstery. Polyether is cheaper in price than latex foam, and is available in various thicknesses and densities, including densities lower than can be obtained in latex. It is therefore possible to choose a suitable foam for almost any requirement. The density is controlled by the chemicals which are mixed when making the foam. Fire retardent grades of foam are also available.

The main defect of polyether is that it offers a high initial resistance to deformation, although once a certain load has been reached this property disappears. This is known as *hysteresis*, and can be described as giving a sudden sinking feeling. These foams have been modified to such a degree that this property is no longer so noticeable.

The chemicals *carbon dioxide* and *urethane polymer* are reacted together no further vulcanizing is then needed as with latex, because after foaming, the polyether sets into its final form. There are two ways by which polyether can be made:

1 *Prepolymer* The ingredients react together before foaming begins. This allows greater control to be kept over the process, which ensures that the polyether will contain the required properties.

2 *One-shot* In this case, mixing and foaming take place simultaneously.

Bonded chipfoam

This is made from reprocessed waste polyether foam which is cut into small granules. The polyether chips are mixed in a predetermined ratio with a precatalysed polyurethane resin in an extruding machine. The resin crosslinks under pressure and sometimes heat, and the chipfoam emerges the same shape as the die at the head of the extruder.

Chipfoam is available from 2 mm ($^1/_{12}$ in.) in thickness. The thinner layers are rotary cut from a cylinder of chipfoam, in which the cylinder is peeled to give a continuous length of chipfoam. It is available in many grades, giving densities up to ten times greater than is possible in polyether foam.

Chipfoam is used in better quality upholstery as a base layer, over which a softer padding material is fitted. It can be used to advantage, together with a moulded rubber edge profile, over a seat spring.

Rubber profiles

These are made from latex and chipfoam and are available with different shaped cross sections for every possible roll and edge application. They can be glued to foam or tacked directly to a frame.

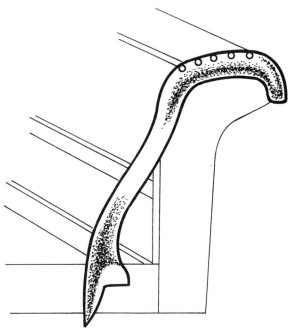

26 Fixing a rubber profile roll around an arm

Fibre

Loose fibre is not used much now in upholstery owing to the time and skill involved in its correct use. Different types are available, each being characterised by colour. *Coir fibre*, also known as *ginger fibre*, is obtained from the coconut husk, and is the most resilient type. It is shipped from Ceylon in bales which are broken open, and the fibre is teased to separate the fibres. A dust extraction system removes any remaining husk and the shorter fibres which add to the bulk but not to the quality of the fibre.

Algerian grass, often called *black and green fibre*, is obtained from the Algerian palm tree and is the next best quality of fibre.

Fibre pads are more convenient to use than loose fibre. These are made by needling a predetermined quantity on to a hessian backing.

Curled hair

This is used as little as fibre for the reasons stated above. It is more resilient than fibre and is much softer to the touch. Hair is usually obtained as a mixture of horse, cattle and hog hair, the proportions depending on price. Horse hair is obtained from the mane and tail and is of better quality than cattle hair which, in turn, is better than hog hair.

The hair is first washed, and a proportion is dyed black. After mixing, the hair is spun into rope, and a curl is set in by steaming or boiling the rope. Heating also sterilizes the hair. After drying, the ropes are stored to allow them to mature. When required, the rope is untwisted and teased, or it is needled on to hessian to make hair pads.

Rubberized hair

This is obtained in sheets of varying densities. It is made by bonding curled hair with rubber latex which is then compressed to the required thickness and density.

Felt

Best quality felt is made from *cotton linters* which are obtained from the waste of the cotton plant after the cotton fibres have been extracted. These linters are pressed into an even layer. Felts can also be made out of rag flock made from processed rags, but this product is not as resilient as cotton felt. To conform to British Standards, the rags need to contain 50 to 60% wool. Felt is used over fibre and hair to prevent fibres from working through the covering fabric.

Polyester fibrefill

This is a recently developed cushion filling material, made in *terylene* and *dacron*, which has contributed enormously to the comfort of seating. It is available as a *bonded batting*, in which the sheets are lightly bonded with acrylic resin on each side, making the material more compact and easier to handle. *Unbonded batting* is also available, in which the fibre-fill is carded and folded into layers, which are then sandwiched between a loosely woven cheese-cloth.

The fibre has good bulking power, and cushions filled with the material are characterised by a full appearance. The fibre is very soft and recovers well from compression. This is due to a new three-dimensional spiral crimp, or a saw-tooth type crimp, which is given to each fibre.

Fibrefill can be used by itself in a cushion or in combination with any type of foam which will blend with the fibre. When a core of foam is being used, cut the foam about the same size as the cushion cover, and wrap the required number of layers around the cushion. If unbonded batting is being used, stitch the cheese-cloth together along three sides for a neater appearance of the cushion. Keep the unsewn edge to the front of the cushion. Bonded batting can be lightly glued to the foam. If a 100% fibrefill cushion is required, use the unbonded batting and fold it to about 25% longer and wider than the cushion size. Use about 1370 gm/m² (4·4 oz per sq ft) in a seat cushion, and 1220 gm/m² (4 oz per sq ft) in a back cushion.

Kapok

This is a vegetable filling material obtained from the seed pods of the kapok tree. It is used in cushions as a cheap substitute for feathers and down. The fibre comes from Java and the Dutch East Indies where it is washed, graded, and compressed into bales for shipping. When it arrives in this country, it is reprocessed by drawing by suction through a hopper, in which the kapok is beaten by arms revolving on an axis. This separates seeds and sand, and expands the kapok into its fluffy and light form.

Kapok is extremely light because of the porous nature of the fibre, but in spite of this, water does not penetrate it very easily. Because of this property it is used as a filling for upholstery in ships, and life-saving equipment.

Feathers and down

These are still used extensively in the more expensive traditional upholstery. Down obtained from the eider duck is more expensive than feathers but is rarely used by itself. Feathers are normally mixed in to give extra weight and to lower the cost. Down contains no large quills and has a much greater filling capacity than feathers.

Feathers are obtained mainly from poultry, much of which is imported from China. Cheaper grades of feathers are chopped to prevent them being felt through the fabric.

Feathers and down are weighed, and then filled by vacuum through a hose into waxed calico cases which prevent the quills from penetrating the fabric. The cases are often divided into three or four separate pockets to spread the filling equally throughout the cushion. The case should be slightly larger than the cushion cover into which it is to fit.

Castors

These are a necessary fitting for upholstery, and much scientific experiment has gone into perfecting different types. The *ball type* is very popular because its patented design ensures almost frictionless and silent mobility. The *mini castor* has a recommended loading of 200 kg (450 lb) on four castors, but the larger version of the ball castor can be loaded to 300 kg (700 lb).

Castors can be provided with different wheels for various floor surfaces, and there are different methods of fixing them to metal and wood frames. There are two main methods. The first is by a *screw plate*, and the second is with a *socket fixing*, where the socket fits into a drilled hole in the frame, and the peg of the castor can be pushed into the socket.

Glides can be fitted to light furniture which does not need wheeling about. They can be fitted by hammering on directly, or by means of a socket.

3 UPHOLSTERY FABRICS

Traditionally, the upholstery fabric market has been predominantly based on a number of fabric types, including moquettes, velvets, tapestries and brocades. Recently there has been a strong move towards the woollen Scandinavian bouclé type of fabric. Acrylic velvets are also being exploited, due to their brightness and the clarity of colouration that they can be given, also to their warmth, softness to touch, durability and easy cleaning properties. The trend has particularly moved away from moquettes.

The choice of fabric is a major factor influencing the success or failure of any job. A well chosen cover can transform a mediocre design into something attractive, but a badly chosen cover can make even a well upholstered chair appear drab. Certain covers which may suit certain styles of upholstery may be unsuitable if used on other designs. A cover should be chosen which fits in with surrounding materials, considering texture, pattern and colour. The amount of wear that is likely to take place must also be taken into account when buying the fabric.

Woven fabrics

1 *Bedford cord* A fabric with ribs running in the direction of the warp. It is made in a plain or twill weave, and can only be obtained in single colours.

2 *Brocade* A finely woven jacquard fabric with a multi-colour pattern. Originally it was a heavy silk fabric with elaborate pattern, made with silver or gold thread. It is made by floating extra coloured threads on the back of a plainly woven ground cloth, which are brought to the surface when required. Brocades are made from cotton, wool, silk and man-made fibres, and have a firm and smooth hard wearing surface.

3 *Brocatelle* This is similar to brocade, but the heavily figured pattern is raised above the weft backing.

4 *Corduroy* A cut pile fabric with ribs running in the warp direction. The weft yarns float on the surface at intervals which are then cut, brushed, and singed to form the pile. It is a hard wearing fabric, made from cotton and man-made fibres, and is in the medium to high price range.

5 *Chintz* A closely woven printed cotton fabric in a plain weave and with a glazed surface.

6 *Crash* A heavy, rough textured, plain woven fabric made from jute, flax, hemp and cotton.

7 *Cretonne* Similar to chintz but without the glazing.

8 *Damask* Similar to brocade, but it is flatter and is reversible. It was originally made in Damascus from where it takes its name.

9 *Denim* A hard wearing coarse cotton twill fabric of low cost.

10 *Genoa velvet* A heavy velvet with a multi-coloured figured pile on a smooth ground. It is a very expensive fabric.

11 *Moquette* A fabric having a pile which is cut, uncut or in a combination of both.

Cut moquettes are made by weaving two fabrics face to face, the pile being formed between, by interlacing both fabrics simultaneously with warp threads. The pile is then cut by a knife which travels between the fabrics. Another method of weaving is by lifting the warp threads over wires which are inserted in place of the weft. The pile is cut by the wires as it is withdrawn.

Uncut moquettes are made with two warps, one of which forms the pile. Wires are inserted in place of the weft, but unlike those used above, they have no cutting edge. After weaving, the wires are withdrawn, leaving a pile in the form of loops.

Moquettes having a combination of cut and uncut pile use cutting blade wires and plain wires. They are extremely hard wearing, can be obtained in many designs in both man-made and natural fibres but are generally very expensive.

12 *Plush* A fabric having a longer but less dense pile than velvet. It is in the medium to high price range.

13 *Repp* A plain woven fabric with ribs in the direction of the weft. It is a very hard wearing fabric, in the medium price range.

14 *Sateen* A fabric in which the weft float over the surface of the warp forming a smooth surface. It can be made without twill lines. The weave is also known as *weft satin*, and is in the medium price range.

15 *Satin* A fabric in which the warp float over the surface of the weft, forming a smooth surface. This weave is also known as *warp sateen*.

16 *Tapestry* A jacquard figured fabric made from part or all wool, with coarse yarns which can be made in a variety of weaves. It can be obtained in many colours and is very expensive.

17 *Terry velvet* An uncut loop pile velvet which is woven over wires similar to the uncut moquette. It is very highly priced.

18 *Tweed* A simple twill weave fabric with a smooth, hard-waring surface. It is usually made from all wool, but other fibres are also used. Due to its simple weave, the fabric is reasonably priced.

19 *Velour* A warp pile fabric with a very short pile.

20 *Velvet* Produced with a double warp, one of which forms the pile. The ground warp is woven with weft yarns through which the pile is woven. A wire with a cutting blade is inserted between the pile warp to form loops, which are cut as the wire is extracted.

Velvets are also made in a similar way to cut moquettes, by weaving two fabrics face to face with the pile between, which is sliced through the middle to separate them. It is very highly priced.

21 *Velveteen* A weft pile fabric. It is woven with floating weft yarns which are cut after applying a paste to the back of the fabric to fix the yarns, so they do not move during cutting.

Knitted fabrics

These are used in woven fabric applications. They are also for covering plastics chair shells because their stretch properties are well suited to fitting around the double curvature shapes associated with these types of chair.

They are liable to damage by loop pulling and laddering, which do not occur so frequently with woven covers. Damage is usually caused during sewing and fitting of the cover. Laddering can be caused by piercing the fabric with sewing needle, tacks and staples. The fabric can also be damaged if too rigid a seam is used for sewing, in which case the fabric might be torn by the thread when it is being stretched during upholstering or use. Foam or rubber backing a fabric lessens the chance of laddering.

1 *Warp knitted fabrics* These can be woven to give an appearance of either ordinary woven cloth or weft knits which are described below. They can be produced faster than woven fabrics, and are used in competition with them. They can be made with raised or unraised loops and can be made ladder resistant (a disadvantage associated with weft knits). They are woven mainly from continuous filament yarns, and different types of surface texture can be produced with either an open or closed structure. Knitting styles vary with different machines, the difference between machines being based on the number of needles and the thickness of yarn which is used. Warp knits are so called because threads run along the length of the fabric.

2 *Weft knitted fabrics* These fabrics have more stretch than warp knitted fabrics. The fabric is made up of interlocking loops of yarn. The loops are formed across the fabric with a single thread. There are three basic types of weft knitted fabrics used in upholstery: *single jersey*, *double jersey* and *interlock*, all of which can be knitted with variations. The former is a plain knitted fabric, and is very prone to laddering. Double jersey has a rib structure, and is so called because the stitches which lie in two planes tend to come together to form a double fabric. Interlock is also a double rib fabric, but it has interlocking cross yarns which prevent the fabric from damaging easily.

Coated fabrics

Rexine made from *nitrocellulose* was the first plastic coated fabric to be used, but has now been superseded by other plastics.

1 *Polyvinyl chloride* PVC fabrics have good abrasion resistance and are easily cleaned. This makes them suitable for both contract and domestic upholstery.

The properties of a coated fabric depend on the backing fabric, the type, content and thickness of the coating material, the adhesion between and the method of application of the coating to the fabric, and the decoration of the surface.

Many types of backing fabric are used for strengthening the coating surface. The cheapest fabrics have no backing, and tear more easily than backed fabrics. *Vynide* has a woven backing fabric having good abrasion and flexing properties. Other PVC materials have knitted fabric backings to give the fabrics greater stretch properties, making upholstering easier.

Expanded and unexpanded PVC are used in making coatings. *Ambla* and *Cirrus* are expanded fabrics which are softer and warmer than plain PVC fabrics. They are made by incorporating a blowing agent which expands the mixture to give a thin layer of foam with an integral skin of solid PVC.

A plasticiser is added to PVC to give the fabric certain properties. The type and quantity used affects abrasion resistance and general flexibility.

PVC fabrics can be obtained in many colours. The amount and type of pigment used affects the light stability of the fabric.

There are two methods of making the coated fabric, both of which use PVC as a *plastisol* (paste).

The *doctor knife method* is the process usually used, in which the paste is spread on the fabric by means of a roller and a doctor knife, which control the thickness deposited as the fabric moves between them on a conveyor. The fabric then passes through a heated oven at 160 to 170°C to gell the coating. An embossing roller imprints the pattern on the surface, and the fabric is rolled.

A second method, *dip coating*, involves passing the base fabric through an impregnating bath containing the paste. Excess paste is removed by rollers. Heating and embossing is carried out as above.

1 *Direct coating* involves spreading the polyurethane as a viscous liquid directly on the base fabric by means of rollers. A thicker and less stretchy fabric is formed by this method.

2 *Transfer coating* is more suitable for lighter coatings, and is applied to knitted fabrics. The coating is applied to a release paper, and is partially dried. The film is then transferred and bonded to the backing. The release paper is usually made from a strong kraft paper, which is coated with release agent to release readily the coating from the paper, and also a resin (polyurethane in this case). The paper can be plain or embossed, depending on the surface requirements for the fabric. The paper acts as a carrier to transport the resin coating on to the fabric backing, after which it is peeled off and can be used again. The general fabric properties depend on the effectiveness of the coating process, and the adhesion and thickness of the coating. This process is also used with PVC.

Polyurethane

These fabrics are more like leather than other synthetics. They are usually applied in a thinner coating than PVC. Like PVC, they are air permeable, have good stain and abrasion resistance, and are easy to clean and upholster with. They can be finished with a matt or gloss 'wet look'.

Glossy fabrics usually contain a two-component finish, and the fabrics are tested to ensure that they will not delaminate through bad adhesion of the two dissimilar coatings. Certain of these fabrics also tend to be sticky.

Fabrics are divided into two groups governed by the method of coating.

Welding of PVC

The sewing of PVC can be avoided in mass production by using a radio frequency heating welding machine. This machine can form quilting patterns if suitable jigs are made, and it can make a seam much faster than a sewing machine. Power output, welding time and depth of sink of the welding blades are the machine's variables, which need to be carefully regulated according to the fabric in order to produce good welds.

The average weld strength of backed PVC is 42% of the fabric strength. Thoughtful designing is needed to ensure that the seam will not be highly stressed.

Hides

After a long absence from modern domestic upholstery, leather is once again in demand as a covering material.

Cow hides of about 3·3 sq m (45 sq ft) are obtained in irregular shapes. They can be squared for easier planning of cutting, but this raises the price of the hide. Hides are bought as whole or half hides. The outer side is called the *grain side*, and the inner side is the *flesh side*. Leather crushes easily, so it should be rolled neatly with the grain on the outside to prevent this.

Joins can be made on hides by skiving pieces together. This is done by cutting the pieces to be joined at an angle so that there is greater surface contact, and then gluing them together.

The warble fly is the major cause of imperfections on a hide, but barbed wire and bramble scratches also cause surface markings. The holes heal on the animal to form scars which do not affect the strength of the leather. Certain blemishes add to the natural effect, while others need to be buffed out.

Hides are first washed, then left to soak in pits containing lime and sodium sulphide. This aids removal of hair. The hides are split into layers, the top layer being used for best upholstery leather, and the bottom or flesh split being used for suede leather. The leather is de-limed, and is passed to the currier in the rough tanned condition. The rough hides are sorted into groups, based on their ultimate use. They are then soaked in water and allowed to equalise in moisture content with the surroundings.

The hides are shaved on the underside to give them a level substance (thickness) before they enter the drum house where tanning is continued by introducing oil into the leather in the form of an emulsion. The hides pass from drum to drum, alternating between cleaning and re-tanning by specially prepared warm liquors. Chemicals are added to guard against rotting.

The hides enter the setting-out machine, which contains rubber rollers between which the hides pass, extracting most of the moisture from the hides. They are transferred to the stretching shop, where they are stretched to facilitate drying. It is not the aim of stretching to make them larger in area. They are dried under controlled relative humidity and temperature to ensure uniform drying throughout their substance.

The hides are now in the *russet state*. Those for use in upholstery are re-sorted before staining. Those selected as *buffed antique hides* are sent to the buffing shop, those for *printing* to the printing shop, and those for *natural full grain hides* are left unfinished.

Stained hides are sprayed with aniline dyes. The colour is rubbed into the grain, the surplus is wiped off, and the hides are dried in an oven. Hides which are unsuitable for a natural grain finish, owing to blemishes, are embossed with an artificial grain. They are then placed in a revolving drum for several hours to produce a crushed effect.

The full grain hide has an undisturbed surface, all natural grain and blemishes being left intact.

A buffed antique finish is given to hides which are unsuitable for other finishing treatments, owing to bad surface markings. The blemishes are removed from the surface of the hide by a machine containing cylinders which are covered with carborundum paper. The hide is then embossed and finished in a similar way to the full grain hide. This type of hide is the cheapest upholstery hide produced.

27   Skiving leather

Trimmings

Self-piping or ruche is often used as an alternative to having plain seams along cushion borders, etc.

1 *Self-piping* consists of piping made from the same material as the covering fabric. The sewing of self-piping is described on page 48.

2 *Ruche* can be obtained in shades to match most covers. One edge of the ruche is suitable for sewing into the seams of the fabric. There are three main types of ruche.
  (i) Cut ruche consisting of a continuous closely woven thread, with a cut pile surface.
  (ii) Loop ruche which is similar, but its pile is not cut.
  (iii) Rope ruche which is made in the form of rope, with decorative threads on the surface.

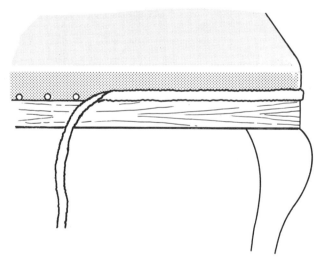

28 Fixing gimp with glue or gimp pins

3 *Braid and gimp* is a decorative band of material which is glued or gimp pinned along the edge of upholstery, particularly where the cover finishes against a show-wood frame.

4 *Upholstery nails* are used as an alternative to slip stitching to finish a job. They are hammered in to the frame at regular intervals, after folding in the raw edge of the material. They are commonly used on plastics coated fabrics which are difficult to sew by hand. Nails can be obtained with a brass or antique finish, or in colours to match a fabric.

5 *Fringe* is gimp-pinned or sewn around the perimeter of upholstered furniture as an added decoration. It consists of loose, twisted threads which hang from a length of braid. It can also be obtained with tassels.

Care and cleaning of fabrics

All upholstery should be cleaned regularly with a vacuum cleaner or a soft brush to prevent dust from settling in the fabric.

When fixed upholstery covers require cleaning, which should not be too infrequently, a special dry foam upholstery cleaner can be bought, which cleans the fabric without damaging the underneath padding.

Most loose fabrics can be taken off and washed by hand or in a washing machine. Fabrics react differently to washing and heat, so the recommended washing and ironing instructions should be followed. If no washing instructions have been given with the fabric, it is safer to consult a dry-cleaner.

Plastics coated fabrics need only to be wiped over with a damp, soapy cloth, followed by a dry duster, in order to keep them looking like new. Polishes should not be used on these fabrics.

Fibres

Fibres from which upholstery fabrics are woven are split into four main types:

1   *Natural fibres* are obtained directly from animal and plant, and include wool, cotton and silk.

2   *Bast fibres* are vegetable fibres, and are obtained from the stem of various plants. These include jute, flax and hemp.

3   *Man-made fibres* are split into three different groups of fibre:
   (i) *Cellulose fibres* are produced by modifying natural cellulose, eg acetate and viscose rayon.
   (ii) *Protein fibres* are made by modifying natural proteins, eg protein from casein and ground nut soya bean.
   (iii) *Synthetic fibres* are produced from polymeric (plastics) materials, eg nylon, polyester, and acrylics.

4   *Mineral fibres*, such as metallic filaments, are often used for decoration.
   The following is a list of fibres with some of their trade names

FIBRE	SOME TYPES AND TRADE NAMES AVAILABLE
wool	*merino, cross-bred, mohair, cashmere, alpacca*
cotton	*sea-island, egyptian (sakel and karnak), pima*
silk	*bombyx mori*
acrylic	*acrilan, courtelle, dralon, orlon, teklan (modacrylic)*
casein	*fibrolane*
elastomeric	*lycra and spanzelle*
metallic	*lurex*

continued

nylon	*antron, bri-nylon, celon, enkalon, perlon*
polyester	*dacron, terylene, crimplene*
polythene and polypropylene	*courlene, cournova, ulstron*
polyvinyl	*darvan, saran*
rayon	*fibro (staple)*
modified rayon	*evlan*

Man-made fibres

These are being used in an ever-increasing quantity for upholstery fabrics. Although wool is still one of the better fibres, its high price is restricting its use, and man-made fibres are necessary to provide wool equivalents at lower cost. Man-made fibres also offer properties which are not available in natural fibres. Each fibre has its own characteristics, and by blending natural and man-made fibres, many desirable properties can be incorporated into a fabric. For instance, the addition of a coarse denier, long staple rayon to wool will increase its strength and abrasion resistance.

Yarns made from man-made fibres can be produced with a lustrous or matt finish, and with different forms of texture, giving different grades of strength and abrasion resistance.

All man-made fibres are produced by taking a fibre-forming substance (a polymer), converting it into liquid form, forcing the liquid through a 'spinneret' having very fine holes, and causing the streams of liquid to solidify as fibres. This process is carried out in different ways, depending on the chemical nature of the fibre.

Man-made fibres are available in two forms: *continuous filament* and *staple filament* yarn. Continuous filament yarn contains from one to one hundred or more individual filaments. The thickness of the yarn is indicated by the denier. Continuous

33

filament yarns are produced from 15 denier to 2000 denier.

Staple fibre is obtained by cutting a thick rope of filaments (a *tow*) into fibres of the required length. 25 mm to 200 mm (1 in. to 8 in.) fibres can be made depending on the spinning system to be employed.

TEXTILE TERMS

1   *Bouclé yarn*   A decorative yarn having loops or knots at regular intervals, and made from two or more threads which are twisted together.

2   *Bulked yarn*   A textured yarn, consisting of a crimped or folded yarn which gives bulk, softness and warmth to a fabric. It is made from man-made fibres to resemble wool. Bulking changes the original fibre properties.

3   *Catalyst*   A substance which is added to speed up a chemical reaction, without taking part in the reaction itself.

4   *Crimp*   The waviness of a fibre. It is found naturally in wool, but it can be inserted permanently into man-made fibres by heat setting. It is used in textured yarns to give bulk.

5   *Denier*   The term applied to filament man-made fibres and silk, and is the measure of thickness of a yarn. The denier is the weight in grammes of 9000 metres of yarn.

6   *Ends*   The term given to individual warp threads.

7   *Filament*   A continuous fibre, obtained after melt spinning a man-made fibre mixture. Filaments are naturally obtained in silk. See *Staple*.

8   *Picks*   The term given to individual weft threads. The number of picks per centimetre (inch) depends on the yarn count and the closeness of the weave.

9   *Plain weave*   The simplest but closest method of weaving.

10   *Selvedge*   Provided along the edges of a fabric to give a firm and strong edge. The selvedge is made by including extra end warp yarns which are either of the same or different but stronger material.

11   *Staple*   Short fibres. A man-made fibre filament can be cut into short lengths to form staple fibres. Natural fibres are obtained in staple form.

12   *Stretch yarn*   A textured yarn which is made to give a fabric elasticity. It is similar to a bulked yarn but has more stretch.

13   *Tex*   A metric system of yarn numbering which, it is hoped, will supersede and rationalise all other methods. It measures the weight in grammes of 1000 metres of fibres and natural or man-made yarns. Different units are used within the system:

> *militex* = milligrammes per kilometre
> *kilotex* = kilogrammes per kilometre
> *decitex* = decigrammes per kilometre.

14   *Twill weave*   This weave produces diagonal lines across the surface of a fabric.

15   *Warp*   The threads which run along the length of a fabric.

16   *Weft*   These threads run across the fabric at right angles to the warp.

34

17 *Yarn count* A measure of yarn thickness. It is calculated by an indirect method of measurement, usually based on the pound unit. This method measures length per unit weight as opposed to the direct method which measures weight per unit length. In the indirect method, the coarser yarns have lower numbers, but by the direct method, the coarser the yarn, the higher is the number. The denier and tex systems work by the direct method.

Weaving

All woven fabrics are produced on a loom. The basic principle of weaving involves holding the warp yarns under tension, and interlacing with weft yarns. The weft yarns are held in shuttles which are sent across the warp threads as required, after raising the chosen warp ends.

Jacquard loom

This loom allows complex repeat patterns to be woven. The pattern of the fabric is transferred to rectangular cards by means of punched holes. Each line of picks uses one card. There are as many cards as there are picks in each repeat pattern. The cards are laced together and fitted in a belt on the loom. Needles are fitted to the loom which come into contact with the cards. Where holes have been punched in the cards, the needles enter, which causes the associated warp threads to be raised. After the weft yarn has been inserted, the needles withdraw and the next card comes into place to restart the cycle.

Another type of loom uses a long strip of thick paper instead of individual cards.

The martindale abrasion machine

This is considered to be the most reliable machine for determining the abrasion resistance of the majority of woven fabrics. Fabrics having certain textured yarns and those with long piles are unsuitable for testing. This test is understood by the average consumer, and salesmen often talk about fabrics having a particular number of *rubs*.

Tests need to be carried out under controlled conditions of temperature and humidity, and an average is found from the results of a number of tests. A figure of 35,000 rubs is considered to be the minimum acceptable number for domestic upholstery fabrics, but results of over 40,000 rubs are necessary for hard wearing fabrics suitable for contract use.

Specimens are cut into 36 mm ($1\frac{1}{2}$ in.) diameter discs, and are clamped into the abrading head over 3 mm ($\frac{1}{8}$ in.) thickness of foam. Four specimens are simultaneously. Specimens should be examined at certain stages to note any change, which can be assessed as follows:

1 The partial exposure of backing structure.

2 Removal of pile from a pile fabric, exposing the backing.

3 Breaking of the threads.

4 Removal of nap from the surface.

5 Rate of weight loss. Specimens should be weighed every 1000 rubs.

6 *Pilling* This is the forming of small balls of fluff on the surface.

7 Testing to destruction. This is not as useful a test as when the fabric is tested for earlier deterioration.

4 STRIPPING AND REPAIRING THE FRAME

See *chapter 1* for the tools required for the stripping operation.

The cover and materials should be stripped in reverse order to the upholstering. The usual sequence is to remove the base cover, followed by the outside back, outside arms, seat, inside back, and inside arms. It is important to remember the order in which the frame was upholstered, and also where trimmings have been used on the cover.

The piece of furniture being stripped should always be in a suitable position for working. To strip the base cover, the frame should be in position (a). Settees can be worked in either (a), (b) or (c), but chairs are more convenient to handle because of position (d) which can also be used.

These positions should be used for upholstering as well as stripping. If certain parts are not being recovered, or the cover is to be replaced after repair to the frame, it is important not to damage the fabric. This can be prevented by resting the covered frame on some cloth or padding, placed on the floor and on the bench.

If the inside springing and padding are in good condition, it might be possible to leave them on the job, if the upholsterer is sure that by doing so, it does not impede the fixing of the new cover. If the padding has been flattened, a layer of felt placed over the old padding will help to build up its resilience again.

The old cover should be saved so that the pieces can be used as patterns for cutting the new cover. Extra cover should be allowed in places where it can be seen that cover has been trimmed from the original piece. Hessian flies should also be fitted where they are thought to be necessary.

The frame can be altered for modernisation of the design. If this is done, the old cover must not be used for patterns, but new measurements need to be taken around the frame after fitting the padding.

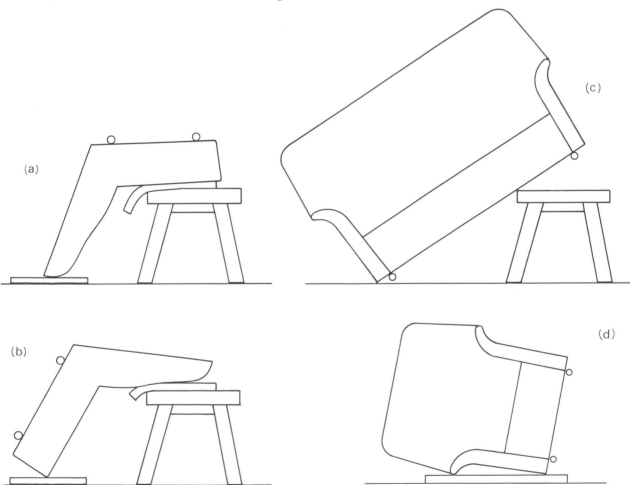

29   Positions used in the stripping and upholstering operations

30 Brace and bit

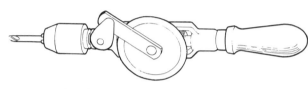

31 Hand drill

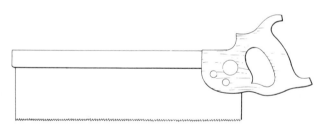

32 Tenon saw

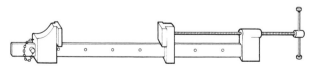

33 Sash cramp

Tools required for frame repairs

Tools not mentioned here will be found in chapter 1.

1 *Brace and bit* This is used for drilling out broken dowels, and for drilling new dowel holes. It is also used for drilling castor holes. The brace can be used with screwdriver bits.

2 *Hand drill* Required for drilling screw pilot holes. These prevent splitting the timber, and also make screwing easier. A countersink bit is also required.

3 *Screwdrivers* These are required if screwdriver bits for the brace are not available.

4 *Tenon saw* This is used for cutting rails to length, for cutting corner blocks, and for cutting off old dowels before re-drilling the holes.

5 *Sash cramps* At least two are necessary to ensure correct setting of a glued joint. If none is available, a length of joined wire can be used with which to improvise. The cramp action of tightening a joint will occur when, with the aid of a lever, the wire is twisted.

6 *Rasp* This is used to chamfer the sharp edge of a rail where there is a danger that the edge will cut through the padding, and make a hole in the fabric. It is necessary to round the inside of rails where rubber webbing is to be fitted, and the edge over which a roll is to be stitched.

7 *Bevel* This tool is useful for measuring angles, such as when marking out corner blocks.

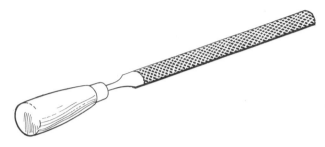

34 Rasp

35 Bevel

Materials

1 *Timber* This should be straight and close grained, with a medium degree of hardness, and free from knots which reduce its strength. The timber should be able to retain tacks, but it should not be too hard to make their insertion difficult. Timber which is too hard also stands a greater chance of being split by tacks.

Beech is usually quoted as being the most suitable for frame construction, but choice depends on availability. Birch, maple and poplar are only three of the many that are available.

2 *Dowels* These can be obtained in a number of different diameter sizes, in either continuous or cut lengths. Dowels, 38 mm ($1\frac{1}{2}$ in.) long with a 9 mm ($\frac{3}{8}$ in.) diameter are a convenient size to use.

3 *Screws* Countersunk head wood screws are used in the construction of frames, as they are not needed to give a decorative effect. Oversize screws might split a rail, so the size should be carefully chosen. 35 mm to 60 mm ($1\frac{1}{2}$ in. to $2\frac{1}{2}$ in.) screws in an 8 gauge are those most frequently used.

4 *Nails* These are often used as a substitute for screws. They should not be used in place of screws or joints, but should only be used in positions where they will not be stressed, such as for the fixing of plywood.

5 *Glue* There are many types of glue on the market for wood joints. Animal glue is very flexible and is a good gap filler, which are the main reasons for its continued use in frames. It is bought in cakes and is used hot, but it should not be allowed to boil. The glue sets on cooling.

PVA (polyvinyl acetate) is gaining ground as a glue for chair frames, but it does not match the properties of animal glue.

Bostik and *Evo-stick* are synthetic glues which are more easily applied. The manufacturer's instructions for application must be followed.

Repairing the frame

1   *Repairing and making new dowel joints*   Dowelling is the most suitable joint for chair construction. The joint stands up well to the battering and flexing to which chair frames are prone.

The number of dowels needed for each joint varies from between one and three, depending on the size of the joint, and the amount of stress it is to take.

Old dowels firstly need to be extracted. If the glue bond has broken, it is easy to pull them out.

Otherwise, they will have to be drilled out. The brace, fitted with a bit of the same diameter as that of the dowel, will prepare a new hole at the same time as it extracts the dowel. The hole should be drilled slightly deeper than half the length of the dowel to allow for excess glue.

Glue should be applied to the dowel hole only. On cramping, the glue will run up the side of the dowel to the joint surface. The dowel should be either grooved all round, or a saw cut should be made down one side of the dowel, to allow an escape route for excess glue. This avoids pressure being set up at the bottom of the hole when the glue is compressed by the dowel, and thus avoids the chance of splitting the timber.

After gluing one set of dowel holes, locate the dowel pins into the holes. Now add glue to the other half of the joint, and connect and cramp the complete joint until the glue sets.

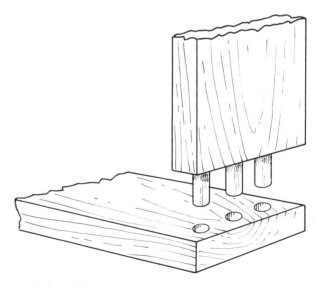

36   A dowel joint

2 *Fitting new corner blocks* New corner blocks should be fitted in the seat if the existing ones are in a poor condition. Nailed blocks should be reinforced with screws.

Cut the blocks with a tenon saw, making slight adjustments to the angles, to ensure a close fit. Drill the screw pilot holes perpendicular to the sawn edge. If castors are to be fitted into the blocks, drill holes to hold the sockets.

Corner blocks can also be fitted to a chair back if the design permits, and if their addition will be beneficial to the back's strength.

3 *Curing other loose joints* A loose joint can be simply repaired by re-gluing and cramping. A few extra screws inserted through the joint at an angle will give the joint extra strength. Drilled and countersunk pilot holes are necessary to insert the screw at the correct angle, and to ensure that the

angled screw heads do not remain above the surface of the rail.

Screws should not be inserted into the end grain of timber because screws do not grip very well from this direction.

4 *Fitting new rails* A broken or weakened rail needs to be replaced by a new one. The timber need not be the same as the rest of the frame. Cut the rail to the size of the old rail, and accurately mark out the dowel holes to correspond with their pairing holes. To fit the rail, it might be necessary to loosen some of the other joints, which will have to be re-glued and cramped at the same time as the new rail is being cramped.

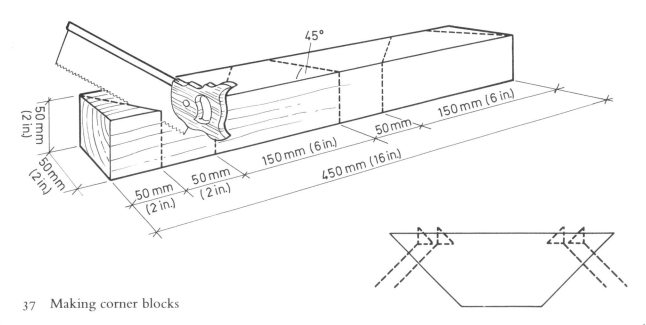

37   Making corner blocks

5 *Frame not symetrical* This is found on new frames which have not been assembled correctly. A small amount of unevenness can be hidden by the upholstery, but a frame which is significantly out of square will need to be re-glued and cramped at the necessary joints.

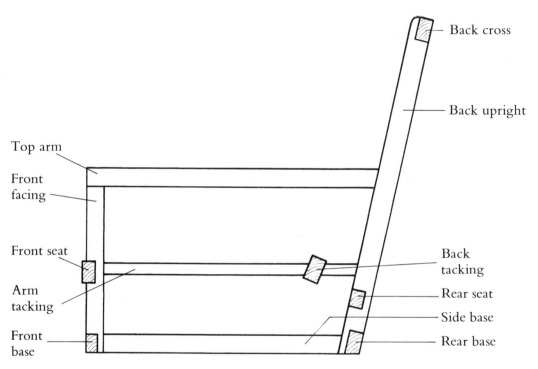

Back cross

Back upright

Top arm

Front facing

Front seat

Arm tacking

Front base

Back tacking

Rear seat

Side base

Rear base

38 Sectional side elevation of a frame

5 SIMPLE UPHOLSTERY REPAIRS

There are various reasons for having to carry out repairs. Below are mentioned a few of the causes, with the required action to be taken.

Broken seat webbing

This occurs on chairs which have been upholstered with hour-glass springs on a webbing base. It is characterised by a sagging seat, which is often thought to have been caused by broken springs.

If it has occurred in the seat, which is the most likely place, invert the chair and remove the base cover. Rip out the broken webbing, after cutting the knots holding them to the springs. Stretch new webbing over the positions of the old webbing, and re-sew the springs to the webbing. For greater detail of the correct methods of fitting webbing and sewing in springs, see pages 59 to 61.

Webbing does not need to be broken before new webbing is fitted. New webbing can also be fitted when the old webbing has gone slack, which also causes the seat to sag. In this case, the old webbing need not be ripped out but should be supported by the new webbing. The springs should be re-sewn to the webbing as before.

Changing castors

This only needs the simple operation of extracting the old castor and replacing it with a new one. Some castors have different size sockets, so it might be necessary to re-drill the hole to make it larger, or a smaller hole might have to be drilled by the side of the existing one. Do not drill into a screw holding a corner block to the frame. Castors can also be changed from socket to plate fixing, and *vice versa*. If the corner blocks upon which the castors are mounted are in bad condition, their repair is discussed on page 41.

Damaged fabric

Fabric is easily damaged. Whether it is done by the family's pet dog or by a dropped cigarette, the requirement is still the same: a new fabric panel is usually needed.

Sometimes, with certain stretchy fabrics, depending where the damage is, it might be possible to stretch the fabric until the mark is hidden. With other fabrics such as moquettes, where threads have pulled, new threads can be carefully sewn in with a slipping needle, the thread being obtained from a piece of fabric in an inconspicuous place such as from underneath the base cover. This latter repair should only be used when a new fabric panel is not obtainable.

To match the fabric, send a pattern to the original manufacturers of the upholstery or the fabric supplier. If the cloth is obsolete, the repair can either be matched with a near shade or pattern, or the upholstery will have to be recovered completely in another cover.

If the fabric can be obtained, it can be fitted directly over the old cover, but it is better to remove the old cover before re-fitting. There is less work involved if the outside back is damaged than if the inside arm is damaged. Fitting inside covers becomes more complicated because other parts of the upholstery need to be loosened to allow for correct fitting. Take off the old cover and use it as a pattern for cutting new cover. Re-fit the cover as described in chapter 12.

6 MARKING OUT AND CUTTING THE COVER

Cover is the costliest material used in upholstery, and thoughtful planning of parts is essential to keep the cost as low as possible.

In a furniture factory the conventional cutting process involves four operations:

1 Collecting the roll of cover from the stores and laying it on the table.

2 Marking with the aid of patterns.

3 Cutting the cover.

4 Sorting and bundling the cover in preparation for sewing.

One cutter can be used to perform all the operations, or the job can be split so that two or more operatives of differing labour value work on different sections of the process. Cover can be cut either singly or in layers. Shears can be used for cutting up to about five layers of cover, but electrical cutter knives are needed for greater thicknesses.

Because the home handyman does no repetative cutting, he needs to measure each piece of cover either directly from the job, or from pieces being stripped for recovering. If possible, an economical cutting plan should be worked out on paper before starting to cut.

The cutting table should be the stage where all the damages in the fabric are noticed. If they are missed at this point, there is a danger that the damaged fabric will go unnoticed until at the final inspection stage of the upholstery when it will be more costly to repair. To prevent this from happening, it is important that the cutting table should be provided with good overhead lighting.

Fabrics having no pile but with ribs running in one direction, can be cut to display the ribs running either down and forwards, or across the job. Lines running downwards tend to make a job appear higher, while those running across make the job appear wider. The latter method usually gives the better effect.

If there is a pile to the cover, cut it so that the pile will run downwards or forwards on the upholstery. Cut a patterned fabric so that the pattern will be displayed to its best advantage. This is usually achieved by centralising the pattern in a panel. Mark out with white or blue tailor's chalk, using a pattern or template. Cut all the large pieces first. Allow a 9 mm ($\frac{3}{8}$ in.) sewing seam where necessary. Slight allowances in size may also need to be made if the fabric is expected to stretch during upholstering.

When cutting settees, joinings will probably have to be made in the length of the back and seat. Cut two equal joining pieces, and sew them to each side of the panel, so that they are equally spaced on the upholstery. Joinings can also be made in piping, borders, etc. Cut strips of cover about 35 mm ($1\frac{1}{2}$ in.) wide for piping.

Advantages and disadvantages of cutting singly and in layers

1 Most manufacturers sell many different designs in a wide range of covers. With this policy there is no scope for cutting in layers. Only if a company can sell a limited number of designs in a set number of fabrics, can bulk cutting be used to advantage.

2 There is not much difference in the time taken to cut one layer and many layers. Therefore labour costs can be reduced by cutting in bulk.

3 Cover usage is usually greater when lay cutting. The plan of the lay should be such that as many straight cuts across the roll can be made, to enable damages to be cut out, and the roll restarted, with the minimum of wastage. Each time a length is cut off and restarted, an overlap allowance of about 25 mm (1 in.) should be made. The piece remaining after cutting out the damage may be inserted between two other straight cuts, if large enough.

The layout must be made for the narrowest fabric being laid up, any extra width being waste.

4 Striped and patterned fabrics are harder to lay up because the pattern on each ply must be matched accurately with the others in the lay.

5 Longer suite-length tables are recommended for laying up, which many factories cannot accommodate. A suite may take about 23 m (25 yd) of cover, and a table of about this length would make it possible to lay the whole suite in one stage.

7 USING THE SEWING MACHINE

Sewing the cut cover in preparation for upholstering is the next stage after cutting.

Stitch type

The usual type of machine stitch used in upholstery is the *lock stitch*. This is formed using a needle thread and a bobbin thread. The thread from the bobbin, which is fitted beneath the throat plate, passes through a loop formed by the needle thread. The amount of thread on the bobbin limits the time when sewing can be continued, before the bobbin needs to be re-wound. The tension on the machine needs to be accurately controlled, so that the two threads meet in the middle of the fabric. If the tension is incorrect, the intersection will occur on the surface of the cover, which is a main cause of fault in sewing.

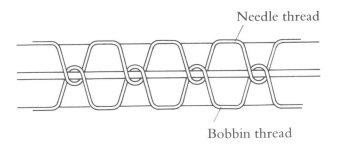

Needle thread

Bobbin thread

39 Correctly tensioned lockstitch

Knitted fabrics

The *chain stitch* and the *overlock stitch* are used on knitted stretch fabrics because these stitches contain strongly looped threads which are flexible to expand and contract with the cover. The two types of stitch can also be incorporated into one stitch, which is known as *stitch type 512*.

These seams require closer stitching than the lock stitch seam, and they use more thread which is put into use during stretching of the cover. Knitted stretch fabrics usually need to be overlocked along the edges to prevent the cover from laddering. Over-locking can also be used on normal woven fabrics, to prevent fraying of the edges. Overlocking is an edge binding stitch which provides a neat finish to an edge, and also trims the edge. Weft knitted fabrics should be overlocked, but this is not always necessary with warp knitted fabrics which do not stretch as much as the former.

Overlock and chain stitches can unravel if one of the threads are broken, which does not occur with the lock stitch. Both types of stitch should be sewn using finer needles than those used for the lock stitch. Synthetic thread should be used as this stretches more than the normal cotton thread.

Machine needles

Heavy industrial machines are used in an upholstery factory machine room, but most types of machine can be used if they are fitted with a needle of correct size, to sew the usually heavy-weight covers. A machine needle size between 16 and 19 should be used on most materials. Plastics coated fabrics, however, are easily cut by a sewing machine needle, so a finer needle between 9 and 11 should be used on these.

Machine adjustments

The stitch length should be adjusted to the weight of the cover. 6 to 12 stitches per 25 mm (1 in.) should be used, the larger stitches being used on plastics coated fabrics and the thinner covers. The tension of the machine should be regulated for sewing different weights of cover and for different types of machine thread. Less tension is needed when using a synthetic thread than when using cotton thread.

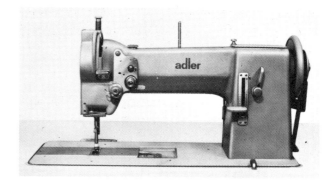

40   Sewing components of a machine

Twin needle machines

Double seams are becoming popular as a decoration. Twin needle machines are available in conventional form and as a post type, in which the throat plate is raised on a column about 150 mm (6 in.) above the working table.

Corners are sewn on the machine by stopping the machine as soon as the inside needle reaches the corner. The inside needle is raised out of the way, and the other needle sews around the corner. Once around the corner, the inside needle is lowered into operation again.

Cotton tape is often dispensed from the underside of the machine as sewing proceeds, to strengthen the seam.

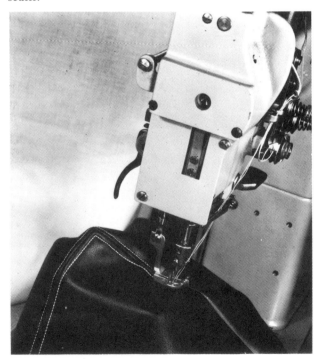

41 Sewing a cushion with a twin needle machine

Twin needling can also be done on a conventional machine by sewing two separate rows of stitches. The sewing must be done accurately because variation in width between the two rows is readily noticeable.

Top stitching *also known as French Seaming and Raising*

This is a further sewing decoration which also serves the purpose of strengthening the seam more substantially than twin needling does. It is sewn after adjusting the seam underneath to one side so that the top stitching will sew through three thicknesses of cover. The sewing gives the appearance of twin needling on one side of the seam only.

Synthetic machine thread

Synthetic thread is more expensive than plain cotton thread, but it is finer, tougher, and more economical in use. Most machine thread used on fabric has a breaking strain of 2·25 kg to 2·75 kg (5 lb to 6 lb), but if necessary, synthetic threads can be obtained which have a breaking strain of about 4·75 kg (10½ lb). This thread gives a machined seam which is normally as strong as the cover itself.

Because it is finer, more thread can be wound on a bobbin, so less time is spent in changing and rewinding it. Also, because of its fineness, less thread is used in stitching. Synthetic thread has better elastic properties which are necessary for knitted fabrics. There are many types of synthetic thread available: *terylene*/cotton thread size 90 (BS 50) and ICI nylon 2/210 denier (BS 60) are suitable for most upholstery stitching.

Twin needling   Top stitching

Sewing piping

Piping can be used on most seams as an alternative to plain seams. A piping foot attachment should be fitted to the machine to simplify sewing. The piping foot enables a seam to be made close to the piping cord.

1 Join the strips into the length required.

2 Lay the cord along the strip on the wrong side of the cover.

3 Fold the cover over the cord and guide the piping foot over the doubled cover, stitching close to the cord.

General hints on sewing

1 When sewing around a corner, cut darts into the seam to make sewing simpler.

2 When sewing joinings, shade the cover, making sure that the pile runs in one direction.

3 When joining two cover panels, notch the centre of each and machine from the centre marks, to ensure that the panels are centralised equally.

4 When sewing hessian flies, turn the edge of the hessian over so that the seam runs through a double thickness of hessian.

5 The sewing of cushions is where most accuracy is needed. Make sure that all corners of the cushion are sewn correctly.

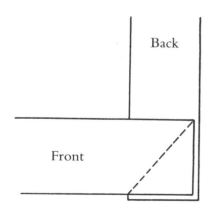

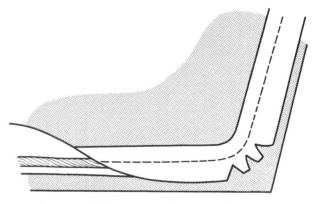

42   Sewing piping to a cushion panel

8 GENERAL UPHOLSTERING TECHNIQUES

Conversion with foam

Latex is often moulded to manufacturers' requirements when the quantity ordered is large enough to justify the outlay for making special moulds. When the number of products is not large enough to warrant this, the shapes are made up by hand cutting and joining pieces together from a moulded block or from sheet. This process is known as *conversion*, but is also called *handbuilding* in relation to latex foam. Cavity, plain and pin core foams are used successfully for conversion and both latex and polyether foams are made in blocks specially for this purpose.

Foams can be marked out with either pen or chalk. When shaped work is being produced, a thin

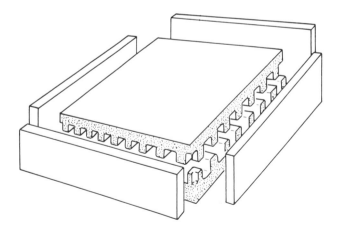

43   Handbuilding a cushion

cardboard pattern should be made, around which the shape can be marked. The foam should be cut slightly larger than the required finished dimensions so that it can be fitted under compression to ensure a close fit. An extra 6 mm to 12 mm ($\frac{1}{4}$ in. to $\frac{1}{2}$ in.) should be allowed on every 250 mm (10 in.) which is cut.

Use a pair of shears or a sharp knife for cutting foams if electric cutters are not available.

Rubber adhesives for bonding the foam should be recommended by the foam manufacturer. Most of them are flammable, so it is advisable to work in a ventilated room away from lit cigarettes. Apply the adhesive to both surfaces to be joined. Leave the adhesive for a few minutes to become tacky, during which time the solvent in the adhesive evaporates. An immediate bond is produced when the two surfaces are united.

Reversible cushions can be built up from two pieces of cavity latex foam. A domed centre can be incorporated by including a piece of 22 mm (1 in.) foam in the centre of the cushion. This should be 75 mm (3 in.) smaller all round than the main cushion. Glue strips of 12 mm ($\frac{1}{2}$ in.) plain sheet around the sides to give the cushion a solid edge. The completed cushion should finish about 12 mm ($\frac{1}{2}$ in.) larger than the cushion cover.

Cushions can also be made with a rounded front by tapering the ends of the two pieces of foam, gluing the two sheets together, and finally gluing the two tapered ends together. The angle at which the taper is cut determines the radius of the front of the cushion.

When a zip is being fitted to the back of the cushion, it is advisable to use a cotton cover between the zip and the cushion. If leather or any other impermeable plastics cover is used, ventilation eyelets or a strip of woven cloth chould be incorporated in the back border.

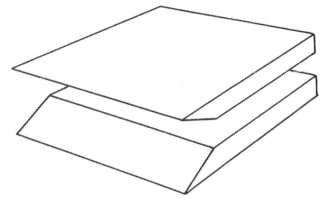

44 Making a cushion with a rounded front

A rounded edge

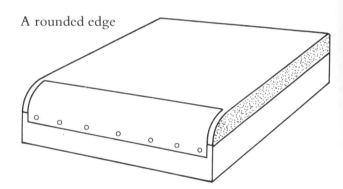

A square edge

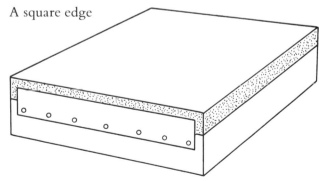

45 Attaching foam to a frame

Foam should be attached to a frame by means of strips of calico, about 150 mm (6 in.) wide which are glued to the foam and tacked to the frame. A neat square or rounded edge can be produced by this method.

Polyether foams can be handbuilt using different density foams in a unit, in order to provide extra support in certain parts of a sheet, such as may be required for the lumbar support on a back.

Back tacking

This is a method of fixing the cover to the frame to produce a clean line without any tacks being visible. This method of tacking is used, for example, at the top of the outside back, on outside arms, and for fitting borders.

Back tacking is done on plain cover and on piped and ruched edges, but extra care needs to be taken over the latter two, to make sure that the trimming is trapped correctly by the cardboard. Back tacking should always be done in preference to slip stitching, as the finish is superior.

The operation is carried out as follows:

1   Place the cover in position, making sure that it is centralised, and about 12 mm ($\frac{1}{2}$ in.) of fabric is folded in.

2   Turn the cover over and tack it in place, keeping the cover tight between the tacks. Place the tacks in the 12 mm ($\frac{1}{2}$ in.) of cover which was previously turned in, but is now in full view along the edge of the cover. It is along this seam that the back tacking is to be done.

3   Cut a strip of cardboard 12 mm ($\frac{1}{2}$ in.) wide and as long as the length to be back tacked.

4   Place the strip over the cover at the required height, and tack the cardboard at closer intervals as near to the edge as possible.

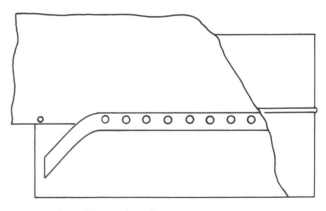

46   Back tacking a border

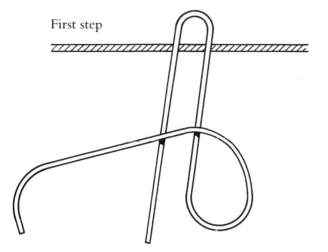

First step

Tying a slip knot

This is the most used knot in upholstery, and it is necessary to learn to tie one. The knot is used for fixing buttons and for starting any type of sewing.

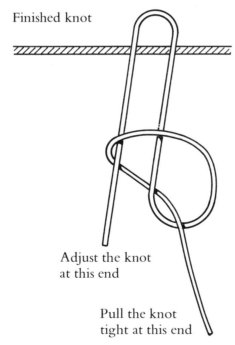

Finished knot

Adjust the knot
at this end

Pull the knot
tight at this end

Slip stitching

This is a method of hand sewing the fabric to finish off the upholstery. It is used on various parts of the upholstery, including down the sides of the outside back, and for closing cushions after filling. Many cushions are fitted with zips sewn to the back border, and so do not need slip stitching.

The fabric is temporarily held in place by tacks or skewers before slip stitching. Special slipping needles are required. See page 12.

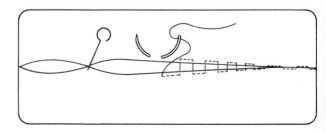

47 Tying a slip knot

48 Slip stitching

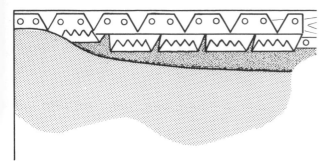

49 The metal strip

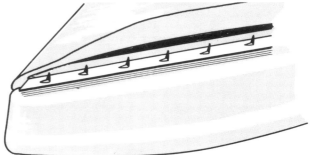

a Place the strip along one edge of the frame

Using the upholstery metal strip

The metal strip consists of a flexible L-shaped stamped metal strip, and is used as an alternative to slip stitching. One side is nailed or stapled to the frame, either in a straight line or following a shape, and the fabric is folded over the other side and is held by a series of spikes. The strip is then carefully hammered together to form the edge.

Using tack trim

Another type of metal strip involving the principal of back tacking is called *tack trim*. This is manufactured from a straight, thin, continuous strip of metal. The points on the strip are cut from the strip and folded outwards. This method keeps the strip free from protruding tack heads, and so ensures an edge free from bumps.

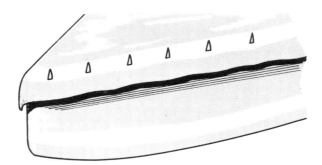

b Press the fabric through the points, and remove excess fabric

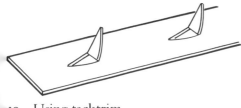

50 Using tacktrim

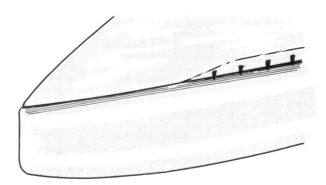

c Turn the strip over, pull the cover tight, and knock the strip into the frame

Buttoning

Buttons can be inserted into either a fixed back or seat. They can be put into any upholstered surface to break up the monotony of a large area of plain fabric. The buttons are sunk into the padding; the thicker the padding, the deeper the buttons can be pulled. Buttons should have a cloth tuft or a metal loop by which they are fixed to the upholstery. Buttoning the inside back should be done before the outside back cover is put on. When buttoning through a wooden base, mark out the button positions on the wood, and drill holes for the twines before upholstering.

1 Measure for the positioning of the buttons, and mark with chalk or skewers.

2 Thread the button through a length of stitching twine or similar thread.

3 Thread the two ends of the twine through the eye of a stitching needle.

4 Push the needle through the cover to the inside of the upholstery. The twine should come through with the needle.

5 Join the two pieces of twine with a slip knot.

6 Insert a tuft of cloth or felt between the knot and the inside stuffing to prevent the knot from pulling through, when the slip knot is tightened.

7 Tighten the slip knot by pulling one of the ends of the twine. Pull the buttons as deep as required. Keep all the buttons at the same depth.

8 Tie off with a reef knot to prevent the slip knot from loosening.

9 Cut off the ends of the twine for neatness.

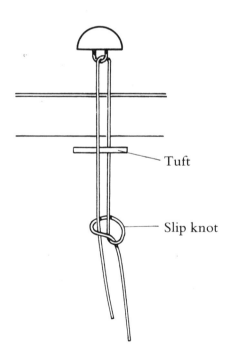

Tuft

Slip knot

51   Buttoning

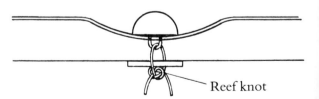

Reef knot

Completed button

Reversible cushions can be buttoned on both sides in a similar manner. Mark the cushions out on both sides. Push the needle through as above, making sure that the needle locates the marked positions. Instead of tufting with a piece of cloth, place a button through one twine and fasten the slip knot around the button. When the slip knot is tightened, both buttons will be pulled in. Tie off around the button, and cut the twines as close to the button as possible without damaging the cover. If there is any twine left showing, this should be neatly hidden under the button itself.

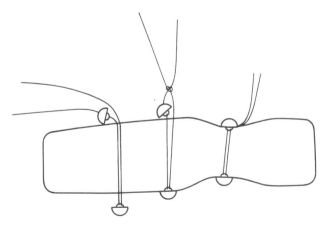

52　Buttoning a cushion

Deep buttoning

This was much used in Victorian chairs, and is used today in upholstering chesterfields and modern designs which incorporate deep buttoning. The old type of deep buttoning, using hair and wadding as the stuffing between the buttons, produced a relatively hard back or seat, but today, foams are usually used in the interior.

The method of deep buttoning with hair and wadding is as follows:

1　Mark out the position of the buttons on the base before stuffing. A diamond pattern us usually used.

2　Mark out the cover, allowing about 36 mm ($1\frac{1}{2}$ in.) extra between the buttons for pleating.

3　Start buttoning from the middle of the panel, stuffing each pocket separately before continuing on the adjacent buttons. Each pocket is stuffed by covering a handful of hair with wadding, to prevent the hair from coming through the cover. Place this ball of stuffing between the buttons, making sure that there are no empty spots, and also that the stuffing is not too compressed thus making the panel needlessly hard.

Pleat the loose cover so that they face downwards or across in one direction only. This prevents the collection of dust inside the pleats. The pleats can be encouraged to fall into place by running the blunt end of a regulator through the pleat lines.

4　Finish the edges of the panel by pleating directly between the end buttons and the outside edge.

Deep buttoning can also be done in latex and polyether foams, as follows:

1 Mark out the buttons on the foam sheet. Punch holes into the foam where the buttons are marked. This helps the buttons to sink into the foam.

2 Mark the cover out in a similar way to (2) above. Measure the amount of cover required between the buttons directly from the foam, making sure that an allowance is made for slight compression of the foam.

3 Pull the buttons in either from the centre or in rows, pleating as progress is made in the panel.

To simplify deep buttoning, instead of pleating the cover, the amount of excess cover between the pleats can be pre-calculated, and this can be sewn together by machine in order to lose the pleats.

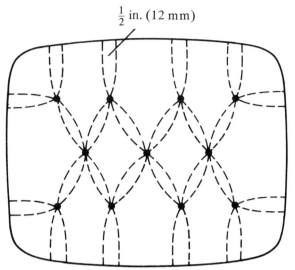

$\frac{1}{2}$ in. (12 mm)

Top cover panel. Sew pleats between button positions

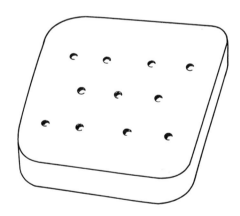

Punch holes in the foam at button positions

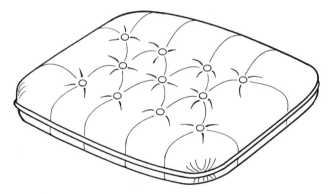

Finished cushion with a layer of *Dacron* over the foam

53 Principle of deep buttoning in foam, as applied to a cushion

Fluting

This is another type of decoration which is used mainly on the inside back over a spring base. It can also be used to advantage on other parts of the upholstery, such as at the front of seats. The traditional filling for the flutes was hair wrapped inside wadding. Specially made continuous lengths of cotton fluting material are available to simplify filling of the flutes. Polyether and latex foams are also used inside flutes. Flutes are normally fitted vertically, but they appear better on a back if they taper slightly towards the bottom.

1   Mark out the positioning of flutes on hessian. There is no set rule for distances between flutes, but 60 to 100 mm ($2\frac{1}{2}$ to 4 in.) can be taken as a rough guide.

2   Mark out the flutes on the fabric. Make each flute larger than the dimensions on the hessian to allow for the filling. If the flutes are to be tapered, cut the flutes separately, allowing extra in the width for a seam and machine them together. Allow enough fabric around the edges for tacking.

3   Sew the cover to the hessian along the flute lines. Pockets will be formed in the cover.

4   Fill the flutes with one of the materials described above. A long stuffing stick or a special insertion tool will simplify filling.

5   Temporarily tack the cover to the frame at the bottom and the top of the flutes, placing a tack in the stitching of each flute. Centralize the flutes accurately. Flutes which are even slightly out of centre are very noticeable. Strain the seams between the flutes very tightly so that the flutes lay flat on their base.

54   A leather, deep buttoned wing chair with a mock back cushion (the cushion is fixed but appears loose) Registered design number 947444

6   Tack off the fabric at the top and bottom of the flutes. Clean out all excess material from the centre of each flute, and pleat it over the seam.

7   Pleats can be encouraged to remain in place by inserting buttons through them. This can be used effectively on an inside back.

8   Tack the sides of the panel.

55   Upholstered chair with a fluted back and seat front. The back, on this example, has a spring unit covered with hessian. The flutes are filled with cotton fluting and are fitted directly over the hessian. The pleats are held in place with buttons.

Fitting facings

Facings are upholstered plywood shapes which are fixed to the frame at the front of the arm. A common example is the scroll arm type. They are fitted either before or after the seat is upholstered, depending on the design requirements.

There are different methods of attaching facings. One method is to fit them by means of nuts and bolts. Another method is to use dowels which are glued to the main frame. A further method is to nail the facings to the frame before padding them.

Most facings are tacked to the side of the outside arm, and the outside arm cover is then back tacked over the side of the facing. Facings normally fit to the full height of the arm, and are tacked underneath the bottom rail. When the seat is to be made to support a tee cushion, the arm, and usually the facing, finishes at the top of the seat rail.

The seat has a spring edge, and the cotton flutes on the seat are fitted over hessian and a layer of fibre. A bottom border has been back-tacked below the flutes

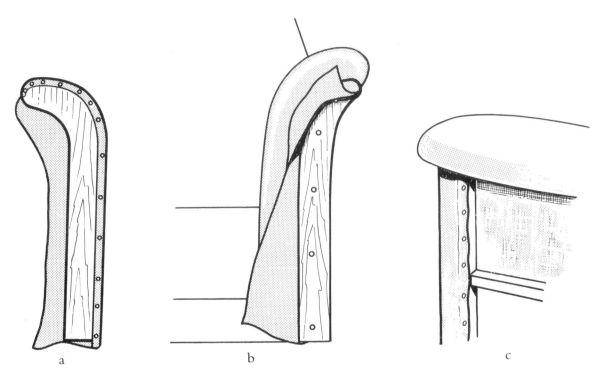

a b c

a   Tack the cover along one side of the plywood facing
b   Nail the facing to the frame before padding with foam or felt
c   Tack the cover at the back of the front arm rail. The outside arm cover is to be back-tacked over this

56   One method of fixing a facing

Webbing a base

Backs and seats which are being hand sprung need to be initially fitted with webbing. Webbing is also applied as a base over other open frames. Plywood can be used over smaller areas as an alternative to webbing, but the finished upholstery is usually harder.

1   Fix the webbing to one end of the rail. Fold the end of the webbing over for strength and tack with 15 mm ($\frac{5}{8}$ in.) improved tacks in a staggered formation to prevent splitting the rail. If the rail is relatively thin, use 12 mm ($\frac{1}{2}$ in.) improved tacks.

2   Strain the webbing to the other side of the rail, using a webbing stretcher to give the correct tension.

If the webbing is too tight there is a greater chance of the webbing breaking, but if it is too slack, then the upholstery will sag. Tack the webbing with three tacks and cut off about 25 mm (1 in.) beyond the tacks. Fold the extra piece of webbing over and tack it with a further two tacks.

3   After fitting the webbing in one direction, fit cross webbings, tacking down as above, and interlacing to give overall support.

Sewing edges

Sewing spring and hard edges is not done by furniture manufacturers, except in special cases, owing to the time and skill involved. Edges can be formed more simply by using rubber profiles which are described on page 24.

A stitched roll is made so that the cover stands upright on the edge, and does not fall away through lack of support. The roll also gives shaping to an edge.

Sewing a spring edge

A spring edge can be built on a seat, a back, or upon any base where a soft sprung edge is preferred to the hard edge described in the next section. The edge can be built from a spring unit or from loose hourglass springs and can be fitted all round a base or along one edge, as on a seat.

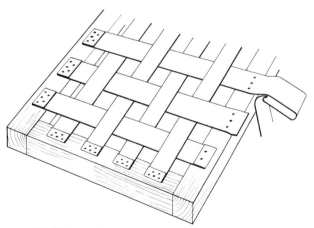

57   Webbing a base

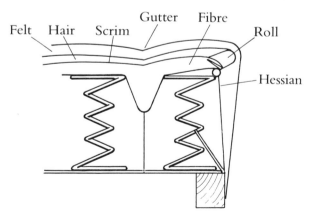

58   The spring edge

1 When hour-glass springs are used, sew them to the webbing base using a bayonet needle and spring twine. Secure them with four knots to every spring. Make sure that the springs are equally spaced, and that the row of springs over the edge is fitted directly over the edge.

2 Obtain a length of spring edge wire, and bend it to the shape of the outside of the frame, leaving extra wire for overlapping where two ends of the wire are to join. The wire can be obtained in straight lengths but a spare spring knocked out of shape will serve the same purpose.

3 Fix the wire along the top outside edge of the springs by lashing together with spring twine or by fixing with metal clips which are bent around the spring and edge wire. Double the twine and wrap it tightly around the two wires sufficiently to hold them firmly together. Knot the twine to prevent it loosening. Do not forget to lash the joining of the wire.

4 Pull the edge springs slightly forward by folding a length of webbing over the middle coil of each spring, and tacking them down under slight tension. This pulls the spring edge wire directly over the front of the rail.

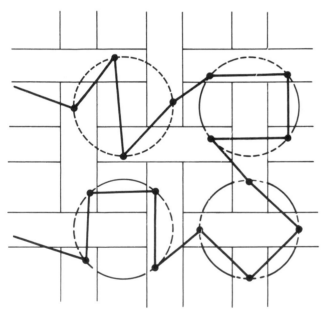

View from behind, showing positioning of knots joining the springs to the webbing

59 Sewing hour glass springs to webbing

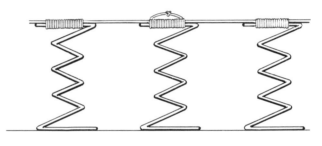

60 Lash the spring edge wire to each spring

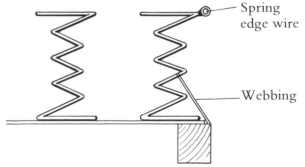

Spring edge wire

Webbing

61 Pull the edge springs forward

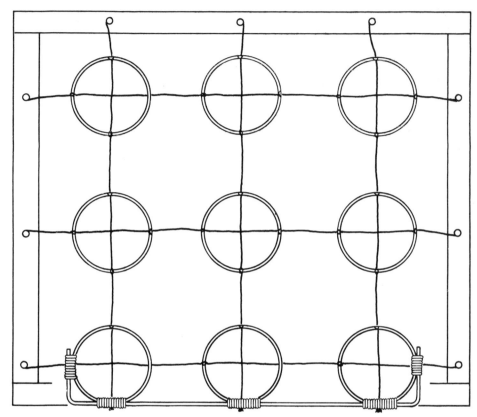

62   Plan view of a seat showing how springs are lashed

5   Lash the tops of all the springs together, preferably with laid cord. Lash from side to side and from front to back to ensure that the springs act as an integral unit. The inside springs should finish in an upright position, but all the outer springs should lean slightly outwards to form a domed shape.

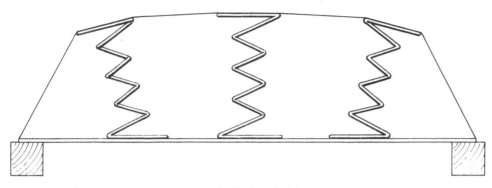

63   Lean the outer springs outwards during lashing

Tack a length of cord to the rail facing each row of springs, or tie the cord to the edge wire. Bring the cord to the top of the edge spring, tie a half hitch at one end and knot the other side of the spring. Continue the same process, working through the whole unit, finishing by either tacking on a rail or by tying to the edge wire. Do not lash directly over where a gutter is to be formed in a seat, but finish the lashing on the spring before the gutter, leaving the front row of springs lashed in one direction only

Continue from here if a spring unit has been used instead of hour-glass springs.

6   Cover the springs with hessian, taking all slackness from the hessian before tacking down. Do not pull the springs down too much over the edge. If a gutter is required in a seat, pull the hessian down between the first and second rows of springs, and hold it in place with twines sewn through the hessian, and tacked on the base. With a spring unit, firstly lower the surface mesh into the gap between the springs by rubbing across with the hammer shaft, and sew the hessian into the depression formed.

7   Sew the springs and the edge wire to the hessian with a circular needle and spring twine. Keep the stitches about 36 mm (1½ in.) apart along the edge wire, and sew three stitches to each spring. This prevents the spring from making holes in the hessian.

8   Sew loops into the hessian to hold the first stuffing. Do not pull the twines too tightly.

9   Coir fibre is usually used as the first or scrim stuffing. Tease it by hand to make sure that there are no lumps in it. Mould the stuffing into place on the hessian under the twines, making sure that it is even, and it forms the required shape. Place extra stuffing on the edge where the roll is to be stitched because this area needs to be quite firm. If a seat has a gutter, pack this with fibre.

10   Cover the fibre with scrim, temporary tacking it to the rail where the edge is not being sewn, but fixing it with skewers where the edge is being stitched. If scrim is not available, hessian can be used.

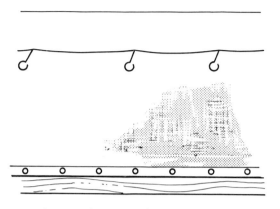
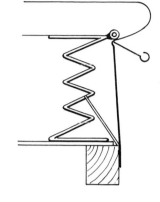

64 Skewered spring edge ready for stitching

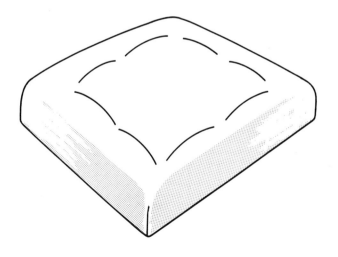

65 The bridle stitch

11 With a stitching needle, sew running through or bridle stitches through the fibre to hold the scrim in place.

12 Re-tack the scrim and re-skewer the edge, folding the scrim under and fixing it to the hessian just below the edge wire. Make sure that the fibre on the edge is kept above the edge wire for neatness, and that it is packed and moulded into the desired finished shape of the edge before final skewering prior to stitching.

13 Stitching is done with a stitching needle and a long length of stitching twine. Blind stitches and top stitches are used, the number of each depending on the type of edge required. One blind stitch and one top stitch is usually sufficient. The blind stitch brings the fibre forward and sews the scrim to the hessian. The top stitch forms the roll.

14 To sew the blind stitch, start at the left hand side (or work anti-clockwise), and insert the needle at a 45° angle from underneath the wire so that it just catches the scrim. Before the twine appears through the top of the scrim, return the needle at a backward angle so that it appears just above the wire and about 25 mm (1 in.) along the edge from the first stitch. Tie the twines together with a slip knot and pull tight. Continue along the edge, pushing the needle through at about 50 mm (2 in.) intervals, and returning it about 25 mm (1 in.) further back from the last stitch, alternating above and below the wire so that the scrim is secured to it. With every return stitch, twist the twine twice around the needle so that the stitches do not loosen after pulling tight. As stiching progresses, remove the skewers from the scrim. After sewing the last stich, tie off with a knot.

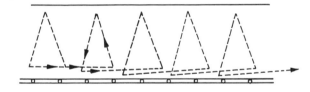

66 Blind stitch

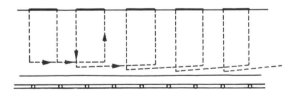

67 Top stitch

Pattern of twine formed during stitching
Twisting of twines between each stitch is not shown for clarity

15 A final top stitch is now needed. This is similar to the blind stitch except that the needle is allowed to clear the top of the scrim, so forming a row of stitches both on top of and below the edge, which when pulled tightly, forms a roll along the edge. The top stitch is kept above and separate from the blind stitch. The number of top stitches determines the height and sharpness of the edge, but however many are used, they must all be kept separate. A roll about the thickness of a thumb should generally be made.

16 Sew loops into the scrim to hold the second stuffing.

17 A good quality hair should be used. Distribute this hair evenly under the loops. The hair should only be used in a thin layer to even out irregularities. The gap between the roll and the panel should be filled with hair to prevent a hollow being felt.

18 The whole stuffed panel can now be covered in calico, which is fitted in the same way as the cover is to be fitted. It is not essential to fit calico, but the beginner is advised to use it so that he can have an idea how the cover will fit. Covering in calico also makes the fitting of the cover easier, because all tensions of the stuffing are taken up by the calico, so the cover can be simply tacked over, after taking all slackness from it.

19 Place a layer of wadding or felt over the calico, to prevent the hair from working its way through the cover.

Sewing a hard edge

This type of edge is similar to the spring edge. It can also be built over a base which is not sprung. When making a hard edge, follow the last section on sewing a spring edge, using the following modifications:

1   The edge is built directly over a rail so that it has no spring.

2   The top of the rail should finish slightly lower than the top of the spring.

3   Do not fit the springs directly over the edge, but space them in from the rail. Do not pull the springs forward with webbing.

4   Without using spring edge wire, tack the hessian over the springs directly on to the rail.

5   Arrange the fibre as above but turn the scrim in and tack it on the top edge of the rail instead of skewering it.

6   Stitch and apply the top stuffing as above.

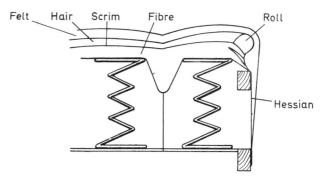

68   The hard edge

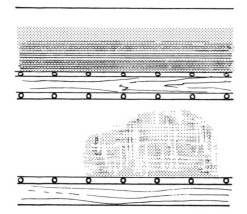

69   A hard edge ready for stitching

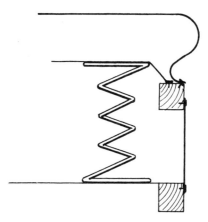

Tack the scrim on the top edge of the rail

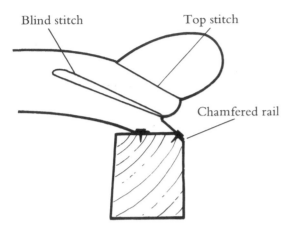

Blind stitch   Top stitch

Chamfered rail

70   Section through the roll

Building fibre rolls

Fibre rolls can be used as an alternative to sewing a hard edge. Prefabricated profiled rolls, made from polyether, latex and compressed paper, are usually used as a more economic substitute for fibre rolls.

Fibre rolls are made as follows:

1   Cut a strip of hessian about 75 mm (3 in.) wide. Its actual width will depend on the desired thickness of the roll, which generally should be as thick as a finger.

2   Turn the edge of the hessian over and tack it to the frame, leaving the loose hessian to face outwards. Pleat the hessian where the roll is to turn a corner.

3   Starting in the middle or at one end, evenly lay in fibre, to form a roll of the required thickness.

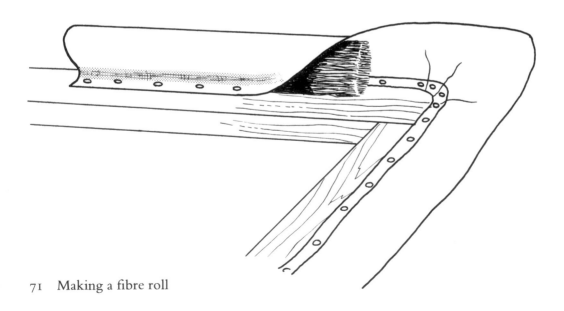

71   Making a fibre roll

Fold the hessian in and tack down, keeping the tacks in a straight line and equally spaced as the roll progresses. Build the roll so that it protrudes over the edge up to about 12 mm ($\frac{1}{2}$ in.). Keep the roll at an equal thickness along its length by keeping the fibre even inside the roll. Prevent tack drags in the hessian by pulling tightly between tacks.

General hints on fixing cover

1   If the cover has a pile, make sure that the pile brushes forward and downward when the cover is fitted. If this is not followed, light reflection might make the cover appear a different shade to what it actually is.

2   If the pattern has been taken into consideration when cutting the cover, make sure the pattern is centralised on the job before tacking.

3   Always keep the lines straight on the cover. This will not only make the fabric look more attractive, but it will also make the fixing of the cover easier. Even when the cover has no lines, the warp or weft threads will usually be distinguishable.

72   Making a V cut

73   Making a straight cut

4 When tacking the cover, avoid tack drags. These are pull lines starting from a tack, which show through in the cover. The type of cover being worked has a great deal to do with their occurrence. Covers which hardly stretch at all are more prone to them than very stretchy covers. Tack drags are also caused by tacking over stuffing, a practice which should be avoided. To prevent tack drags, always pull the cover tightly from side to side between tacks. Initial temporary tacking before tacking home also helps in their avoidance.

Cutting cover to fit around a rail

Cover often has to be fitted around either a tack rail or a show wood rail on a frame.

Fold the cover back so that the fold just touches the rail and cut as shown. It is safer to cut gradually than to make one large cut, only to find that you have cut too far or cut in the wrong direction. It might be necessary to repeat a V-cut on both sides of a rail.

Pleating a square corner

This type of corner finishes with a single pleat.

1 Pull the cover around the corner, and tack it on the edge, on the side of the rail yet to be tacked, within 50 mm (2 in.) of the corner.

2 Cut the cover to take all excess material from the inside of the pleat, to prevent a bulk of cover at the corner, and to allow the pleat to fall in to place easier. Do not cut as far as the top of the corner otherwise the cut may show. Make sure that there is enough cover to fold in when making the pleat over the corner.

3 Finish the pleat, making sure that the cover is not loose. Leave the corner plain or slip stitch along the pleat.

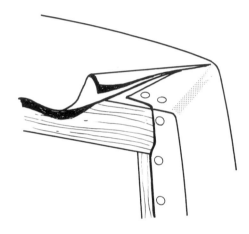

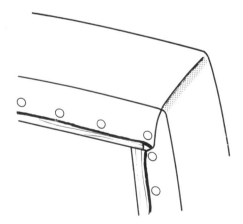

74 Pleating a square corner

69

Pleating a rounded corner

This corner is finished with a double pleat.

1   Pull the cover directly over the corner and tack it at the back of the rail, leaving an equal amount of excess cover on both sides of the corner.

2   Make a pleat on each side of the corner, as close to the corner as possible. Face the pleats inwards to the corner. Cut out excess cover between the pleats, making sure the cuts do not show.

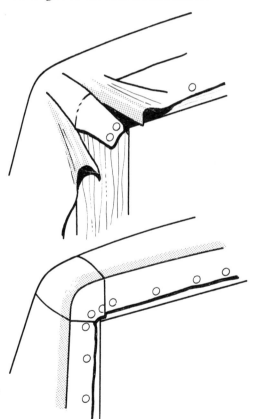

75   Pleating a rounded corner

9   UPHOLSTERING DINING CHAIRS

Dining chairs are fitted with either loose drop-in seats or fully upholstered seats. They also have either upholstered or show wood backs.

A loose seat

These come in different shapes and sizes, and there are different ways of upholstering them. They are based on open frames which may be fitted with a plywood base.

It is essential to remember when upholstering loose seats, to keep the sides of the frame free from stuffing, so that the seat fits accurately into the chair frame. If the seat frame does not closely fit into the chair, the sides can be altered by either tacking cardboard strips on the sides of the frame or planing the sides down.

Mass production of loose seats is usually done using the loose-seat machine described on page 13.

1   The first method of upholstering involves using traditional materials. If plywood has been used on the seat, it is better to replace this with a webbing base which will give a more comfortable seat. Two webbings stretched on the top of the frame in each direction is ample for most sizes of seat, but larger seats may need extra straps. Tack the webbing as described on p 59. Cover with hessian, tacking on a double edge. Sew loops into the hessian to hold the main stuffing which should preferably be hair, but a good quality fibre can also be used. Spread the stuffing evenly over the seat under the loops, building a crown in the centre. The seat can be

covered in calico, prior to fitting the cover, if this should be desired. Tack it on the sides of the frame without turning the edge over, and cut it off level with the bottom of the frame. Cover the seat with a layer of wadding or felt.

2   The seat can be upholstered with a sheet of latex or polyether foam on webbing and hessian, plywood, rubber webbing, or no-sag springs. Tack the foam to the sides of the frame by means of strips of calico which are glued to the foam. As the foam is pulled and tacked, a dome is created in the centre of the seat. See *Conversion with foam*, page 50.

3   Some kitchen chairs have thinly upholstered loose seats made in plywood. Do not use much stuffing on these; a layer of felt might be sufficient. Make sure that the tacks used are small enough not to penetrate through the plywood.

The cover now has to be cut out. Take the measurements from the seat. Make sure that the pile will brush foreward, and that any pattern will appear central on the seat. Allow enough cover so that it can be tacked underneath the frame. Place the cover on the seat and temporary tack it all round. If the corners of the frame are sharp, knock the points down with a hammer because otherwise they might cut through the cover. Finish the corners with a double pleat as described on page 70. The pleats should not be visible when placed in the chair frame. Hammer all tacks home and fit a base cover as described on page 90.

A fully upholstered seat

Fully upholstered dining chair seats can be sprung in a variety of ways, or they can be upholstered without any form of springing. Below are some different methods of upholstering this type of seat.

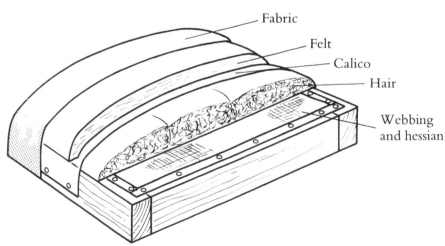

76   Section through a loose seat

1 This method involves the traditional stuffing and stitching of a hard edge as described on page 66. Fix the webbing to the bottom of the seat rails. About three or four stretched in each direction should be enough. Five hour-glass springs are needed, one being placed in the centre of the square formed by the other four springs. Stuff the seat and stitch on all four sides as described. Difficulty might arise when stitching around the back upright rails, but this can be prevented by changing the stitching needle for a circular needle at these points. Add the second stuffing, cover in calico, and cover with felt.

2 Attach rubber webbing to the top of the rail. Cover the straps with 25 mm (1 in.) sheet polyether foam. Glue strips of the same foam to the sides of the chair. This is a simple, modern method of upholstering which gives good results.

There are many variations that can be used in upholstering this seat, and the choice of method will be governed by the materials that are available and the type of result that is required. The methods described on page 73 can also be adapted to this type of seat.

The seat cover can be cut in one piece, or a top panel and side borders can be cut separately, and then sewn together with a plain seam or with a trimming. Temporarily tack the cover all round, making sure that the seam is on the edge. Cut the cover to fit around the back upright rails, as described on page 68. Fold in the cover and gimp pin along the edge of any show wood rails. Pleat the cover where the front and side borders meet. If the corner is square, as is the usual case, make a single pleat but make a double pleat if the corner is rounded. Fit a base cover as described on page 90.

A fixed back

There is a large variety of types of dining chair backs, ranging from the type which just acts as a support for the lumbar region, to the one which covers the whole of the back. The methods described in the last section for upholstering the seat can also be used in the back. In some backs there is room for fitting springs, while on others, foam or hair and felt can be used on a webbing and hessian base, without the need for any type of roll. Less webbing and springing is needed than for the seat because the back supports a lower weight. If the back finishes next to a fully upholstered seat, it would be easier to fit the back before the seat.

Temporarily tack all round on the back of the rail. Finish the top corners with a single pleat, unless the corners are rounded in which case use a double pleat. When the back is set correctly, knock all temporary tacks home. Fit an outside back if necessary as described on page 90.

Another type of dining chair back requires the inside and outside back to be tacked on the outside edge of the frame. The edge is then covered with gimp.

See also *Inside back*, page 86.

10 UPHOLSTERING STOOLS

Most dressing table and foot stools are similar in shape, but vary in dimensions only. The legs of a stool may be straight, splayed, or of the cabriole type. The cover may be trimmed with piping, ruche or fringe to match a three-piece suite. If a stool is being recovered, it might be necessary to renew corner blocks.

Methods of upholstering

1 If the tacking rails are high enough, hour glass springs can be used to build a seat using traditional methods. Fix webbing to the bottom of the rails. Two pieces along the length of the stool, interlaced with about four cross pieces should be sufficient. Use four to six springs, depending on the size of the stool. Form a crown in the centre of the seat with the second stuffing. Do not allow any stuffing to hang over the edge at the bottom of the stool. For greater detail of this method, see *Sewing a hard edge* page 66.

2 Fix webbing and hessian to the top of the rails. Tack a fibre or prefabricated roll around the outside edge of the stool. Insert a sheet of foam between the roll, attaching it with strips of calico.

3 Fix the webbing, hessian and roll as above. Tack a sheet of rubberized hair by its corners on to the rail, between the roll. Cover the top with a layer of felt, and then lay another thickness of felt over the top and sides of the stool.

4 Attach rubber webbing, webbing, or serpentine springs to the top of the rail. Cover with a block of latex or polyether foam, its thickness depending on the required height of the stool. Cover the sides of the stool with either foam or felt.

Covering the stool

1 The simplest method is to cover the stool in one piece of fabric. Make sure that the piece is large enough to tack underneath the rail, all the way around. Temporary tack the cover on all four sides. Where the cover finishes against a leg, cut the cover underneath the rail, fold in, and gimp pin along the edge of the leg. Make a single pleat at the corners, and slip stitch them. See *Pleating a square corner* page 69.

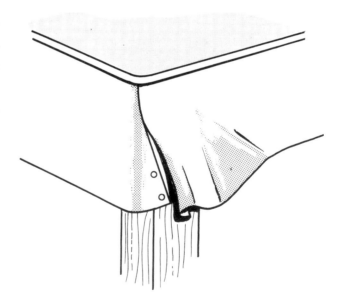

77 Fitting the corner of the stool

2 Cut a top panel and four borders, allowing 9 mm ($\frac{3}{8}$ in.) for a seam. If the stool is to be piped, cut strips of cover about 36 mm ($1\frac{1}{2}$ in.) wide, and slightly longer than the perimeter of the panel. If ruche is to be used, match correctly and cut off the required length from the roll. Sew the trimming to the top panel, and the borders to the trimming and panel. Make sure that the corners line up with the corners on the frame. When fitting the cover,

the seams on the corners may need to be opened from the bottom, in order to fit the corners correctly. Slip stitch the corners together on completion.

Fit a base cover as described on page 90. Fringe can be slip stitched to the base of the stool. Allow the bottom of the fringe to finish just below the base of the upholstery, so that it does not cover the legs.

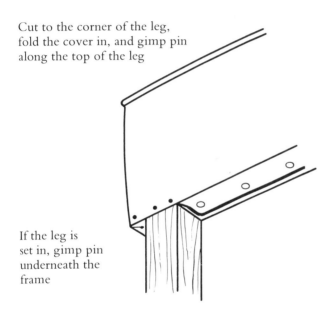

Cut to the corner of the leg, fold the cover in, and gimp pin along the top of the leg

If the leg is set in, gimp pin underneath the frame

78 Fitting cover around show wood legs

79 A traditional stool upholstered with a pre-fabricated roll and polyether foam

11 UPHOLSTERING AN OTTOMAN

An ottoman is a storage unit having an upholstered lid which is also used as a seat. Ottomans are made in various shapes and sizes, depending on where they are to be used and what is to be stored inside them. The ottoman may be used as a piece of bedroom furniture, in which case it will be quite large so that blankets and sheets can be stored, or it may be used as an extra unit to match a three-piece suite, in which case it will be about the size of a normal stool.

The lid, box and base are upholstered separately, and are then assembled using hinges, and a chain stop to prevent the lid from swinging too far back. Before upholstering, check that the frames fit accurately together. The bottom of the ottoman can be finished with small feet or castors. The finished height of the unit should be about 380 mm (15 in.).

Upholstering the lid

The seat or lid is usually upholstered over an open frame. The methods described in chapter 10, page 73, apply to upholstering the lid. Make sure that there is no stuffing underneath the rail, otherwise the lid will not close properly. The cover can be applied as a single piece, or with separate side borders. Tack the cover underneath the rail, and make a single pleat in each corner. Fit a base cover as described on page 90. Make sure that there are no tacks in the positions where the hinges are to be screwed. Slip stitch the pleated corners of the seat.

Lining the box

The square or rectangular box can be made either as a framework or in solid timber. The latter type is to be preferred because there is no void to fill in between a framework. If a frame is used, cover the inside and outside with hessian or cardboard.

Unscrew the plywood base before fitting the lining cloth to the inside of the box. Fabric is not required on the inside. Padding the inside is also unnecessary.

Cut four pieces of lining cloth, slightly larger than the inside dimensions of the box. Fit the lining to the two longest sides first. Tack it to the bottom of the box, over which the base will later be screwed. Strain the lining to the top, and tack it on the inside of the box, within 18 mm ($\frac{3}{4}$ in.) of the top. Tack the ends to the adjacent sides of the box. These tacks will be covered by the remaining two pieces of lining cloth.

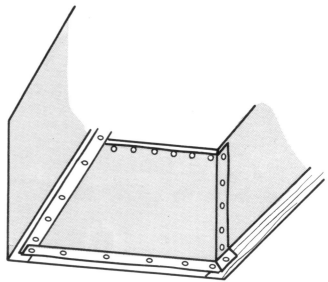

80   Lining the box

Now tack the other two pieces to the ends of the box, tacking the top and bottom as before. Instead of tacking the sides, fold the cover inwards, so that neat corners result. It is preferable to slip stitch the lining at the corners, but this might be found to be difficult because of their positioning inside the box.

Fitting the base

Cut another piece of lining cloth large enough to fit over the base. Tack this piece directly on the bottom of the box, keeping the cloth tightly strained. Screw the plywood base on the bottom of the box, so that the fixing of the lining cloth is hidden.

Upholstering the outside of the box

Cut four pieces of cover, slightly longer than the length and width of the outside of the box, and about 100 mm (4 in.) larger in height.

METHOD I

Fit the two longest sides first. Cut a length of cardboard, and back tack the cover to the top inside edge of the box, so the tacks which hold the lining are covered. Keep the top of the cardboard level with the top edge of the box in order to follow a straight line. Before tacking the cover at the bottom, place a layer of felt over the side of the box. Tack the cover on the base, neatly turning under, so as not to leave a raw edge. If this is done carefully, a base cover is not needed. Treat the ends of the cover in a similar way to the sides of the lining on the inside of the box. That is, tack the ends of the cover on to the adjacent sides of the box.

Tack the remaining two panels of cover in the same way as the first two were attached. Pull the

sides tight, and fold the cover in on the corners of the box. Slip stitch all four corners.

METHOD 2

Sew all four pieces of cover together making sure that the seams fit snugly over the edges of the frame. Pull the cover over the padding. Back tacking cannot be used, so either fold in the edges and gimp pin, or use a metal back tacking strip. Tack the bottom of the cover as above.

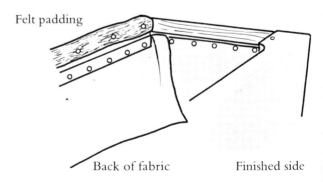

Felt padding

Back of fabric   Finished side

81   Upholstering the outside of the box

Decorative variations

The top of the seat and the sides of the box can be buttoned. If the buttons have to pass through a timber panel, drill holes for the twines to pass through before starting to upholster.

An upholstered border can be fitted around the sides of the box. Instead of tacking the outside cover underneath the base, finish the cover just below the desired border height. Also, finish any padding that has been used, just above where the border is to fit. Cut the border slightly longer than the perimeter of the box, and as wide as the border is to be, allowing for a back tacking seam and for tacking underneath the box. Back tack the border, keeping it level all round. Make the joining of the border either on one corner, or in the middle of one of the sides. Fold the edges in, and slip stitch the joining afterwards. Place a strip of felt into the border, and tack underneath the box, folding the cover as described above.

Fit castors, hinges and a chain stop, to finish the ottoman.

82   This ottoman, shown in the open and closed positions, was made to match a suite

12 UPHOLSTERING SETTEES AND CHAIRS

Upholstery is still traditionally used in the form of three-piece suites, containing a two, three, or four seater settee and two chairs. Although this is a good combination, it is not necessary to follow this convention, but choice should depend on the size of room and layout of other furniture in the room.

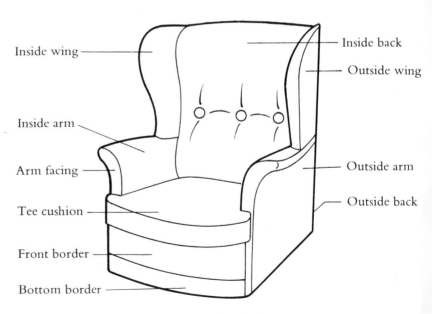

Inside wing

Inside back

Outside wing

Inside arm

Arm facing

Outside arm

Outside back

Tee cushion

Front border

Bottom border

83   Chair cover description

Sectional upholstery

Upholstery can be obtained in units or sections. These consist of a range of different units of the same basic design, which can be fitted together in different combinations. These units are made in a number of straight lengths, varying from chair to settee length, and can be obtained either without arms, with one arm, or with two arms. Curved armless units are also made so that curves can be introduced into a length of seating. Units are also made with a D-end shaped seat, as an alternative finish to using an arm at the end of a unit.

The upholstering of all these units follows the same principals described in this chapter, but the cutting of the cover, especially on the curved units, should be accurate, and should follow the shape of the frame. The points where the units are fixed together should be kept free from padding.

Part assembly upholstery

This method of assembly is sometimes used in mass production, in which arms, backs and seats are upholstered as single units which are bolted together after upholstering.

Upholstering is simpler and faster by this method, and cleaner upholstery lines result. Frames are usually more complicated, because extra rails for bolting are required. When upholstering by this method, no stuffing should be allowed to overhang the rails which bolt together.

84   Sectional suite consisting of four units
      Registered design number 941960

Lining the arms

The first step, when upholstering any type of job, is to line the inside arms. Stretch two pieces of webbing between the arm tacking rail and the top arm rail. Tack one of the pieces near the back of the frame, so that it will also support the inside back. Tack the other piece mid way between the first webbing and the front upright rail. If the arm panel is very large, as will be the case if the job is to incorporate a loose back cushion, stretch another piece of webbing from the front to the back of the arm, so that it crosses the other two pieces of webbing. Pull the webbing tight by hand. Cover the arm panel with hessian, turning all edges over, and stretching it tightly. Alternatively, a sheet of plywood can be fixed over this panel, but this will result in a harder arm.

If the arm being upholstered is the cap-on type, the outside arms should also be lined with hessian. Tack the hessian along the top outside edge of the arm. Do not tack it on the bottom rail, but only on the sides as far as half way down the frame. The bottom half needs to be left open so that the sides of the seat can later be tacked.

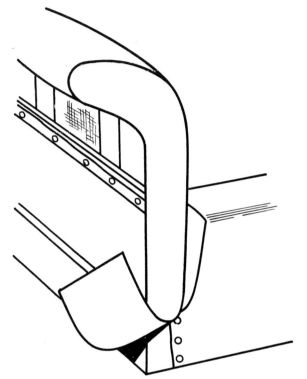

86   The bottom of the arm facing is tacked after finishing the side of the seat

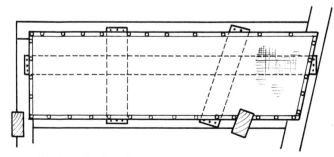

85   Lining the inside arm

80

Upholstering inside arms

There are many different types of arm, but most of them fall into one of the categories below. Arms can be upholstered either simultaneously, or one after the other.

When tacking the front of the arm, it is usual practice to leave the cover loose along the front border, near the bottom of the arm, where the cover meets the front of the seat. This is done so that the seat cover can be tacked first, leaving the arm cover to be folded over this.

1   *Scroll arm*   This is basically a traditional feature, but it is used effectively in modified forms. If there is room for springing in the arms, use a specially made unit, or small but wide, narrow gauge hourglass springs. Serpentine springs can also be used. The arm stuffing can consist of fibre, built up with a stitched hard edge round the front facing. See *Sewing a hard edge* page 66.

Rubberized hair or polyether foam can be used as the main stuffing. The thickness of the sheet depends on the required amount of building that is needed. Before fixing the foam, tack a fibre or prefabricated roll around the front of the arm, allowing the roll to hang over the front of the frame by about 18 mm ($\frac{3}{4}$ in.). Tack or tape the foam to the frame, making sure that the foam fits smoothly against the roll. Do not let the foam hang below the bottom of the arm tacking rail. Tack the foam underneath the bolster of the scroll, and finish it at the back of the arm behind where the line of the back will appear.

Cut and sew the cover for the arms. Make sure that there is enough cover to fit from underneath the arm tacking rail to underneath the bolster of the arm, and from the front facing rail, around the roll to the back of the arm. Sew hessian flies to the bottom and back of the cover. The front of the arm

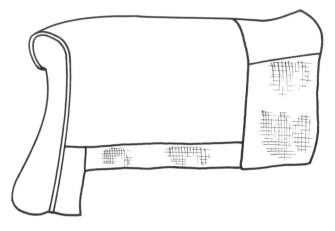

87   Arm cover sewn with flies

88   Chair having loose seat and back cushions with a deep buttoned effect. The arms and wings are sewn in one piece, and cap on to the frame

81

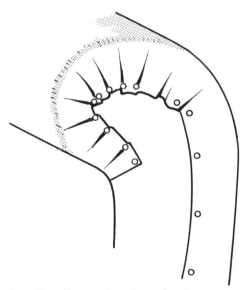

89 Scroll arm showing pleating around the facing

can be sewn with a separate border, and a trimming of piping or ruche.

Temporary tack the cover all round, making sure, if there is a front border, that the seam is directly over the edge on the roll. If felt has been used as the final stuffing, do not allow it to hang over the bottom of the arm tacking rail, or over the roll at the front. Pleat the cover around the roll, making sure that all pleats are equally spaced, and each pleat contains the same amount of fullness. Do not tack the pleats loosely; otherwise, they will not remain in place. Tack home the rest of the arm cover. Now

90 Chair designed and made by the author consisting of a loose back cushion rebated within a top roll

attach a separate loose facing to the front of the arm. See *Fitting facings* page 58.

Separate outside arms will be fitted later, near the end of the job.

2 *Pullover arm* This is upholstered similarly to above, the main difference being in the shape of the front facing. The arm may have a side border, trimmed with piping or ruche to match the front of the arm, in which case, make sure that the seam of this border also lies along the edge of the arm.

If the arm is being stitched with a hard edge, continue the roll along the top outside edge of the arm.

3 *Cap-on arm* The inside and outside arms on this type, are sewn together, with a border separating them. The seams can be plain or trimmed. Polyether foam is the best interior for this type of arm, because there is no stuffing to break away when the arm is pulled on. Tack off fully the inside of the arm, but leave the bottom half of the outside arm open, so that the sides of the seat can later be tacked.

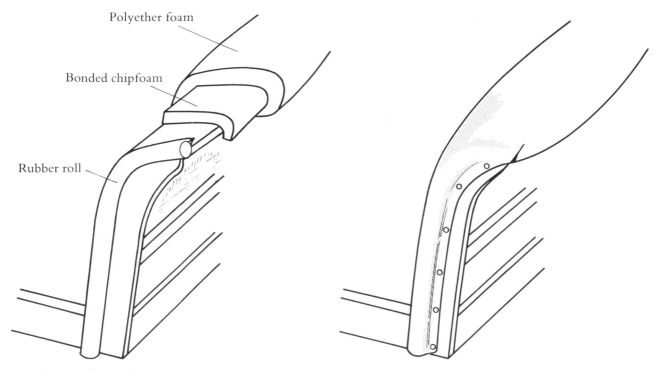

Polyether foam

Bonded chipfoam

Rubber roll

91   Section through a pullover arm

92   Finished arm ready to accept a facing

4 *Arm incorporating a show-wood pad* Decorative arm pads are used quite often at the front of arms. Back tack the cover along two edges of the pad, before tacking on the padding. Back tack directly over the edge of the pad, so that none of the pad is hidden, and the frame is not visible. Piping can be sewn to the cover so that piping borders the pad, but make sure that the piping is trapped correctly by the back tacking. Finish the arm in the usual way.

Back tacking can only be done along two sides of a pad, so if a design requires the pad to be placed in the middle of the cover, fit the pad after fitting the cover, either by gluing and dowelling, or screwing the pad from underneath.

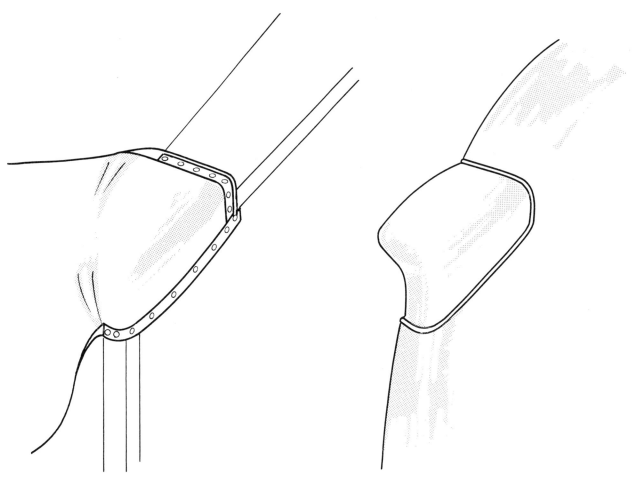

93   Back tacking around a show-wood arm pad

Finished arm

94 Chair incorporating an afromosia arm pad
    bordered with piping
    Registered design number 911196

Inside wings

Wings are sometimes attached to the inside arms,
in which case they will be upholstered at the same
time as the arms. Separate wings are usually fitted
before fitting the inside back.

1   If open frames are used for the wings, cover the
gap on the inside and outside with either hessian or
cardboard.

2   Polyether foam is the best interior filling to use
on inside wings. It should be 25 to 50 mm (1 to 2 in.)
thick, depending on the type of wing being upholstered. Tack or tape the material to the edge of
the frame.

3   Cut the cover for the wings. Shape the cover
along the bottom so that they fit neatly against the
arm. Sew a fly down one side of the wing, for
tacking on the inside of the frame. It also might be
necessary to sew a collar for fitting next to the arm.
Collars are dealt with in the following section *The
inside back*, page 86.

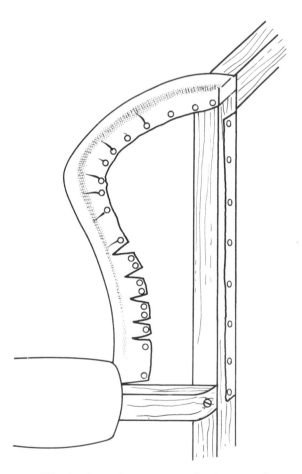

95 Work the wing cover, pleating, and cutting
    darts where necessary

4 As long as the lines on the cover are kept straight, there should be no trouble in fitting the cover. Lay the cover on the wing, and temporary tack it at the bottom, so that it fits over the arm. Cut the cover to make it fit around the top stretcher rail. Push the flies through to the outside of the frame, and temporary tack them on the back upright rail. Now tack the front of the wing cover on to the back of the wing frame. Where the wing curves, cut darts and make pleats in the cover, so that it can be fitted neatly and tightly. Hammer all temporary tacks home.

Fit smooth side to the front

96 Prefabricated chair back in polyether foam

Inside back

The inside back can be plain and upholstered thinly if its sole purpose is to support a back cushion. Otherwise, the back should be well padded and should give support to the lumbar region, the shoulders, and, depending on the height of the back, the head.

There are two main types of back. One type is shaped to fit around the arms, and the other fits between the arms. Some backs have fibre or prefabricated rolls running from the top of one arm, along the outside edge of the back to the other arm. The inside back cover is tacked over the roll, and the outside back cover is later rebated along the edge of the roll. Backs can also be fluted or deep buttoned. Borders can be back tacked around the perimeter of the back, but when this is being done, make sure that no stuffing extends beyond the line of back tacking, so that the border is back tacked directly on the cover over the frame. Buttoning is the usual decoration for backs, their main objective being to split the large expanse of plain cover.

Settee backs can be upholstered as one unit, or with two, three or four separate backs, depending on the size of the settee. Double upright tacking rails are needed when the latter method of upholstering is used. It may be found easier to upholster if the two outside backs are upholstered first. Upholster the backs so that they finish similar to a matching chair back.

The following points should be remembered when fitting most types of back:

1 Backs can be sprung with any of the spring systems which are described on pages 16 to 21. Spring units, hour-glass springs and serpentine springs need to be covered with hessian, but the others can be fitted with polyether foam directly over the spring-

ing. A hard edge can be sewn around three sides of the back using fibre and hair, as described on page 66. Rubberized hair, fibre pads, felt and polyether foam are the most used materials in a back. Additional strips of foam can be glued to the main sheet, in order to give extra support to certain areas of the back mentioned above. Use enough padding so that the springs cannot be felt through the cover.

2 Cut the cover so that the back can tack underneath the back tacking rail at the bottom, and on the back of the top rail at the top. Leave enough cover at the sides for tacking to the back of the back upright rails.

Where the back is shaped to fit around the arms, sew collars to the cover. These are strips of fabric, about 50 mm (2 in.) wide, which are sewn to the back cover, and when fitted, lie over the arm. Sew flies along the other side of the collar.

The back can be fitted with separate side and top borders, which are sewn with a piping or ruche trimming, to give a mock cushion effect.

3 Temporarily tack the cover on the bottom of the back tacking rail. Strain the cover to the top, and tack on the back of the rail. Push all flies through, tacking to the appropriate rails. If the cover is positioned neatly, hammer all tacks home.

See *A fixed back* page 72.

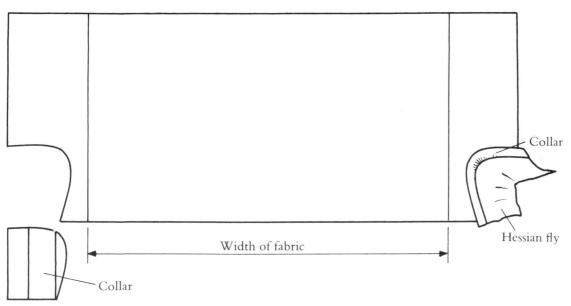

97 Settee inside back showing joins and collars

Seat

All fully upholstered chairs have loose seat cushions. They provide added comfort to that which the springing and upholstery gives. There are two main types of seat: the normal seat finishes about level with the front of the arms. The other type supports a tee cushion. That is, the seat is extended foreward from the front of the arms, and the extension on the seat finishes level with the outside arms. The depth of the seat remains the same as on a normal seat, but the length of the arms are reduced to allow for the protruding sides of the seat.

All seats should have a gutter, to prevent the cushion from sliding off the seat. The gutter should be about 150 mm (6 in.) from the front of the seat.

1 Use any of the springs which are mentioned under the section dealing with the back, but they should be capable of supporting a greater weight than the back. Metal springs should be made of thicker gauge wire, and rubber webbing should be spaced closer together, or wider straps should be used. See pages 16 to 21 for fitting the springing.

2 If a spring or hard edge is to be stitched, stuff the seat and stitch the roll along the front edge only. See pages 60 to 66. Another traditional method of upholstering is to stuff the seat after sewing the cover to the gutter as in (4) below.

3 If rubber webbing or tension springs have been used, it is not essential to use any hessian or padding on the platform of the seat. Polyether foam, chip foam, and fibre pads can be used over the seat. Do not cover this padding with felt yet. The front edge of the seat should be fitted with some form of roll, which can be glued to the front of the padding sheet.

4 Use either lining cloth or normal covering material for the platform. This is the part of the seat between the gutter and the back of the seat. Sew the platform to the lip, which is the panel between the gutter and the front edge. Sew the lip to the front border, either with a plain seam or using a trimming. The lip and the front border can also be cut in one piece without any seam. When measuring for the cover, do not forget to allow for the padding. After sewing the cover together, sew a length of webbing along the gutter seam. Leave an extra 150 mm (6 in.) of webbing on either side of the seat, for tacking down. Sew flies along the sides and back of the platform.

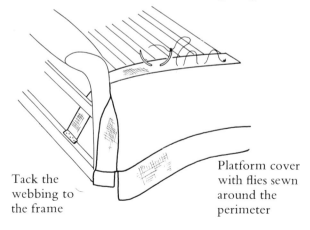

Sew a strip of webbing, or a double thickness of hessian along the gutter seam

Tack the webbing to the frame

Platform cover with flies sewn around the perimeter

98 Sewing a gutter

5   Place the cover on the seat over the padding. Adjust the gutter line on the cover into position, and tack the ends of the webbing on the bottom side rails, after pushing them through the sides of the seat. Fold back the front or rear of the seat so that the webbing is visible. Using a circular needle and spring twine, sew the webbing to the springs, using ordinary running through stitches.

6   Place a layer of felt over the back of the seat, if it is required, and tack the platform cover to the frame by the flies which should be pushed through to the outside of the frame. Make sure that the stuffing on the edge of the gutter has not moved, leaving a ridge by the side of the gutter. Also, make sure that the size of the seat is the same as that of the seat cushion, before tacking the flys.

7   Now finish the front of the seat. Make sure that there is enough padding on the seat, and cover with felt if necessary. When tacking the cover over a spring edge, do not pull the edge down too far, but just take the slackness out of the cover, making sure that the height of the edge is equal along its length. Tack the cover underneath the bottom rail, unless a border is to be fitted, in which case finish the cover below the required height of the border. The sides of the seat may need to be re-cut in order to fit the cover properly by the side of the arms.

8   Back tack a border at the same height, along the length of a seat. Make sure that there is no seat stuffing underneath the back tacking. Piping or ruche can be incorporated in the back border. Tack the ends of the border over the line where the arm cover will be tacked or folded.

9   Tack the front of the arm over the seat if necessary. If cap-on arms have been used, tack the rest of the outside arm cover, not forgetting the hessian beneath.

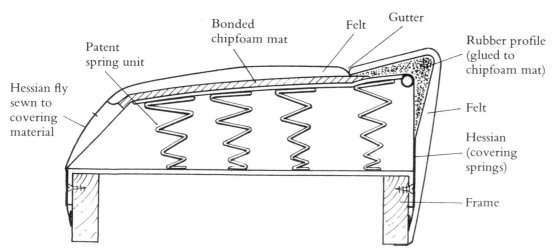

99   Section through a fully upholstered seat

Outside arms

Outside arms can be either tacked without having any reinforcement underneath, or they can be lightly padded by tacking a piece of hessian underneath the outside arm cover, and then laying over a piece of felt.

The usual method of fitting outside arms is to back tack the cover along the most convenient side, which will either be at the top or front of the arm. Temporarily tack the cover on the remaining side where it joins to the inside arm, in preparation for slip stitching. Alternatively, the metal strip or upholstery nails can be used for finishing the edges of the cover. Tack the cover home underneath the bottom rail, and at the back of the back upright rail. Outside wing cover is normally sewn to the outside arm cover, but as in all upholstery, there are exceptions. Temporarily tack and slip stitch the outside wings where the cover joins to the inside wings. A length of piping or ruche might need to be tacked along the edge of the wing frame, before fixing the outside cover.

Outside back

This is always the last piece of cover to be fitted. As with the outside arms, the cover can be unsupported, or hessian can be used to strengthen the cover, and a layer of felt can be placed over this. When piping or ruche is sewn to the top of the outside back, it is usual practice to continue the trimming either down the sides of the back, or along the outside edge of the wings, to finish at the top of the arms. Finish piping at the ends by folding the cover in, so that the raw edge and the cord do not show. Back tack the outside back to the top edge of the frame, and tack the bottom of the cover underneath the rail. Finish the sides by any of the three methods used in the last section.

90

Base cover

It is more convenient to tack on the base cover when the job is upside down. Use calico, hessian or lining cloth. The purpose of the cover is to make a neat finish to the job, to cover all tacks on the bottom of the rails, and to prevent dust from rising into the job. Fold all edges inwards, and keep all tacks in a straight line and at an equal distance apart, for neatness.

Finishing off

The last job is to fit the castors. See page 26 for types and methods of fixing. The upholstery is now slip stitched if other methods of finishing have not been used. See *Slip stitching* page 52. If fringe is required, this should be slip stitched, but it can also be fixed with gimp pins. Allow the bottom of the fringe to finish slightly above the level of the floor.

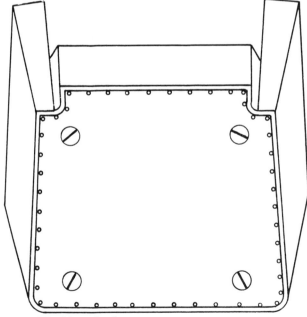

100   Tacking the base cover

SUPPLIERS

The first and simplest place to look for suppliers is in the yellow pages of the telephone directory under 'Upholsterers Supplies' and 'Upholsterers Warehousemen'. Although many of the firms listed will normally supply to the trade only, they are usually willing to help the individual upholsterer and student.

INDEX